Power in the Helping Professions

POWER

in the

Helping Professions

Adolf Guggenbühl-Craig

Translated from the German by
Myron Gubitz

Spring Publications, Inc.
Putnam, Connecticut

Classics in Archetypal Psychology 2

Published by Spring Publications, Inc.
28 Front St. Suite 3, Putnam, CT 06260
(860) 963-1191   Fax: (860) 963-1826
e-mail   springpublications@hotmail.com
secure online bookstore   www.springpub.com

Printed in Canada.

Library of Congress Cataloging-in-Publication Data
Guggenbühl-Craig, Adolf.
Power in the helping professions.
Translation of: Macht als Gefahr beim Helfer.
1. Psychotherapist and patient.
2. Power (Social Sciences).
3. Psychotherapy. I. Title.
RC480.8.G83 1986 616.89'14   86—17901
ISBN 0-88214-304-2

ACKNOWLEDGMENTS

I wish to thank Myron Gubitz for translating this book from my German typescript into an English edition and Patricia Berry for editing. The German language edition appears under the title *Macht als Gefahr beim Helfer* and is published by S. Karger, Basel, © 1971, all rights reserved.

A. G.-C.
June 1971

CONTENTS

FOREWORD
by John R. Haule

I

More than a quarter of a century has passed since *Power in the Helping Professions* first appeared. In that time it has become one of the most influential books to have emerged from the school of psychoanalysis that owes its inspiration to C. G. Jung. Not only are there few Jungian analysts who have not familiarized themselves with it, it has become required reading in many schools of medicine, social work, and professional psychology that otherwise wish to have nothing to do with Jung. For all that it is a humble book, offering little in the way of concrete answers but daring to raise questions the "helping professions" of medicine, psychotherapy, social work, teaching, and the ministry tend to suppress.

The book's author, Adolf Guggenbühl-Craig, M. D., psychiatrist, Jungian analyst, is a powerful man—and not simply because he has held many prominent positions within his profession. Furthermore, as readers of this book will soon learn, he is a man who speaks unorthodox common sense with a confidence based on decades of experience. Evidently his lifetime of work in the helping professions has not been limited to learning his patients' problems but has inspired probing reflections upon his own issues.

We would not be wrong in guessing that one of the most difficult issues he has faced has been dealing with his patients' projections. Somewhere along the line he has had to learn to deal with the fact that people invariably see him as powerful and are apt to attribute more to him that he actually is. By their doing so, he has encountered a problem we all face, a difficulty built into the structure of our profession that cannot be avoided or circumvented with a clever technique. He urges us neither to fight nor to bask in the unrealistic images our clients have of us. Rather we are to accept them like the sunshine and rain of the natural world. Projections are natural facts of interpersonal encounters that simply appear when they must. In the best Socratic sense of knowing nothing in advance, we ought to wait and see what our clients will do.

I have long thought of this as the "Guggenbühl style," although reports from many of Jung's associates indicate that Jung had practiced analysis in much the same manner. Our projections are natural facts of our unconscious life. When they turn the therapist, teacher, or minister into a figure of power—a magician, judge, or prophet—a counter-projection is nearly impossible to resist; and we members of the helping professions inevitably respond to the helplessness, childishness, and longing for mentorship in our patient, student, or parishioner. Some form of the helper/helpless archetype has entered the field between us. Allowing these natural facts to play themselves out is essential if the full conscious/unconscious reality of the encounter is to be respected. To oppose them is to repress the unconscious dynamics of the interchange. It does not annihilate them; it rather forces them to influence our meetings blindly.

In several seminars at the Jung Institute in Zürich during the 1950's, Jung urged his students to be "natural, spontaneous, open, and undefended by the professional persona."

FOREWORD

On one occasion an Italian candidate asked whether this would not allow the analyst's shadow to enter the field. Jung responded immediately: "Well, of course!" The shadows of members of the helping professions will be present. Either we can admit them into our work consciously, observe them, and learn from them; or we can "hide behind our professional persona" and force the shadow into the role of destroyer.

This is the theme of *Power in the Helping Professions.* The more we strive to be professional helpers who have the best interests of our clients at heart, the more we are in danger of acting out of our power-hungry shadow. As soon as we know "what's best" for our patient or student—we have in Guggenbühl's language "split the archetype." One of us is all knowing and all-powerful, and the other is ignorant, neurotic, and powerless. An unconscious drama is then played out in which the helper, clothed in the persona of selfless concern, unconsciously asserts the will over the client. At the other pole of the interchange sits the client, clothed in a compliant persona while unconsciously resisting the helper's domination and belittlement.

Such is the structure of every meeting between the helper and the helped. It is not just an occasional problem and cannot be dismissed as implying an insufficient training on the part of the helper. It is always there. In a series of short, vivid chapters, Guggenbühl makes it clear that there is no way out of this dilemma. Additional training, supervision, and therapy merely exacerbate the situation. The only honest and effective way of dealing with it is to follow the "Guggenbühl style" of professional assistance and consciously admit the shadow into the interpersonal field.

Reading *Power in the Helping Professions* will set us back and humble us. There is no lack of theory or compelling examples. But like every "classic," the book moves us deeply and stays with us because it articulates the living and complex experience of the author. It is based on what really happened and not what should have transpired but did not. Without writing an explicit autobiography, Guggenbühl lets us into his own struggles with the power drive. In the last analysis, this is what reaches us, gives us pause, and sets us to reevaluating our experience as helpers.

II

There are two ways of reading this book. Perhaps most will read it as I first did, attending to the examples and allowing ourselves to be upset by arguments we only dimly grasp because they run so counter to what we would like to believe about ourselves and our profession. In this way of reading, we encounter one shock of recognition after another. We may go through a period of confusion as we try to reconcile our loftiest hopes with the book's unflattering realities.

For example, in addressing the power-shadow of the teacher, Guggenbühl asks what would move and fascinate an individual "to spend his entire working time among children." When the teacher "splits the archetype" and becomes "only a teacher," the students are forced into being childish individuals who do not wish to learn and have no self-control. The teacher becomes the knowing adult facing an unknowing child and has lost touch with her own childishness. This depiction of the teaching profession occasioned a powerful shock of recognition for me. I had taught before and was prepared for all the dodges and lamebrained excuses my students would be sure to use on me. Several "grandmothers" could be expected to "die," and their bereaved grandchildren would need to be excused from their assignments.

To relieve myself in advance of being placed in the moral dilemma of deciding the truth value of such alibis, I borrowed heavily from the wiliness I later projected onto Guggenbühl and constructed a set of rules for my classes that rendered all childish evasions ineffective. There were no deadlines. There were only "suggested completion dates." No penalty would be imposed for failing to meet them. Assignments completed after the suggested date would be given full credit—although late submission also relieved me of my obligation of turning in a grade to the university records office. The student would receive an "Incomplete" for the course, but this would be remedied as soon as the requirements were met. Needless to say, I was rather proud of myself. I did not have to deal with a single alibi that semester, but I found the gap between the teacher's podium and the students' desks a nearly unbridgeable chasm.

At that time I was just beginning to work with my first analyst, where I was being confronted weekly with the imperious way my parents had raised me, and I gave no thought to my difficulties in teaching. Then I had a dream. I was standing in front of my students as the bell rang for the beginning of class, when in walked a tiny, wrinkled woman, as old as the hills. She walked to the front of the room and gestured for me to have a seat with the students. She would teach us all, professor and student alike.

I knew immediately what this dream portended. I had been treating my students with the same imperious power-shadow that my parents had used on me. They, too, had invalidated every alibi in advance, choking my individuality and forcing me into childish compliance, guilty rebellion, or (my favorite tack) sly detachment. Thus it was hardly surprising that I found my students to be slyly detached, rebelliously silent, or childishly compliant. Somehow I had to let the Wise Old Woman into the classroom and rediscover my own childlike enthusiasm for learning. Today, twenty-two years later, I am still teaching and still pondering this dream, trying to find a way to turn my teaching into an extended dialogue with the Wise Old Woman in which I am as much a student as the people in my class. When I am over-prepared and too much in control of my material, she turns sadly away. Only when I place my notes to one side and remain open, spontaneous, vulnerable, and unprotected by my teacher persona does she enter the room and share her wisdom.

The second way of reading *Power in the Helping Professions* is to attend to the structure of its argument. We allow ourselves to be led step-by-step into the depressing reality that there is no escaping our power-wielding shadow, and one-by-one we consider the various strategies that are available to us as helpers. One is the social worker/inquisitor who wants the best for his resisting client while "an uncanny lust for power lurks in the background." He dreams he runs over her with his car and is afraid that he did so intentionally. Another is the medical doctor who genially refuses to accept the powerful projections of his patients. Aha, we think, at last, a humble man! But Guggenbühl brings us up short with an unexpected observation:

> The petty, tyrannical doctor . . . is better than the jovial healer who no longer even takes the trouble to dominate his patients. This cheerful, relaxed fellow has either repressed one pole of the archetype so severely that it can no longer be projected, or else he has

never really been concerned with the basic
problem of the physician and his choice of
profession was merely superficial.

Here we are confronted with the ineluctable paradox of
the "Guggenbühl style." Evading the helper/helpless archetype terminates the healing process. We would be better
off identifying with the shadow and mowing our patient
down with the engine of our ambition. For this, at least,
allows the archetype to appear in the field between us and
our patients. It is the wounded/healer archetype which
alone does the work. Better that it should be neurotically
present than absent altogether. As always, Guggenbühl
knows why he is here. He is shameless in his "political
incorrectness" and urges it upon us all. The "politically
correct" are bland, shadowless helpers who in the end
provide little help of any sort.

On the other hand, the tyrannical helper maintains the
archetype in its split form. The therapist is powerful, wise,
and whole, while the patient is weak, foolish, and frag-
mented. Somehow the Wise Old Woman has to be invited
into the room, revealing to the healer his hidden
woundedness and to the wounded her inner healer. The
split is overcome only when therapist and patient end their
exclusive identification with a single pole of the helper/
helpless archetype. As helpers, we end the polarizing and
empower our patients when we become acquainted with
our power-shadow and realize that there is a very well
established "hook" for the patient's projection. We are not
simply selfless and loving helpers. In knowing "what's best"
for our patients, we tyrannize them with our good intentions. Behind our benevolent persona, a ruthless shadow
is letting out the clutch.

We have arrived at the chapter entitled, "Is Analysis Condemned to Failure?" The problem is that "the more conscious a psychotherapist becomes, the more unconscious he becomes; the more light is cast upon a dark corner of the room, the more the other corners appear to be in darkness." By "coolly tracking down the destructiveness in his patients," he "cuts off access to his own." Overcoming the split requires the therapist to be affected by the patient, to observe how his own unresolved issues are stirred up by the patient's problems. In this way, the Old Woman is allowed into the room, and the therapist is "in the soup" with the patient.

Aside from a few patients who get under our skin and bring our shadows humiliatingly into play, it is not easy for a therapist to enter the unconscious "soup." Even when it happens inadvertently by catching us off guard, it sets off all the alarm bells protecting our professional persona, and we scramble to restore our awareness of the patient's pathology. We reassert our power position as the one who knows better. The very openness, naturalness, and vulnerability we need is experienced as a shameful defeat. We feel disempowered, incompetent, and a failure. Thus the Wise Old Woman's opportunity is precisely our greatest fear. It is the reason Guggenbühl's chapter questioning whether analysis *must* fail is followed by "Analysis Doesn't Help" and "The Helpless Psychotherapist." Analysis and supervision are the therapist's *métier*—training that beam of consciousness into one corner or another and leaving the rest in relative darkness. Furthermore, they are based on the very same power differential that is the problem.

Guggenbühl's conclusions are not pessimistic, but they are tough and humbling. "The psychotherapist must be challenged by something which cannot be either mastered or fended off by his analytical weapons and techniques." This is more difficult than it may seem, for we have known since Freud that the analytic mentality is a powerful thing. It can reduce history, art, literature, mythology, and even science to subordinate positions within its own worldview. The therapist will never enter the "soup" stirred by the Great Woman until he meets something that cannot be mastered.

The honest and humble therapist will find that there is no lack of such forces in her life. But they are rarely to be found in the consulting room. They take the form of the individuals of equal power that we face in our daily lives outside our therapeutic meetings. They are our spouses, siblings, lovers, and friends, the people who will not permit us to manipulate them with our techniques. Another shock of recognition occurred when I was driving my family to New York one weekend years ago to visit my in-laws when my ten-year-old son piped up from the back seat: "Dad, you always ask such innocent questions, but only a fool would answer them." The little guy had my number.

Here is the problem in a nutshell. We members of the helping professions are so habituated to mastering every manner of incident from the lofty position of a comprehensive worldview that we are in danger of reducing our families and friends to "interesting cases." It takes a strong, self-confident, and determined individual to survive as a friend, spouse, or child for those of us who spend out working lives acquiring the persona strategies of our office as professional helpers. The humiliations of family life and friendships provide the arena where our power-shadow can be confronted in all its sly imperiousness. Here is where we find ourselves in the "dark corners" of our psyche. Here is the "soup" that we live in when we turn out the lights in our consulting room and rejoin the world of our bumbling humanity. The stubborn recalcitrance of our loved ones is the voice of the Great Woman. Unless we become acquainted with the shadow we impose upon them, there is no hope for us when we meet with clients.

III

One of Jung's close associates tells an unflattering story about the famous man. There was a large dinner party, and Jung was silently devoted to his food, as was his wont, when another analyst at the table began to speak of his difficulties in analyzing a young boy. Jung immediately perked up and began asking the man questions. Mrs. Jung listened quietly for a while before breaking in irritably: "Carl, you don't give a damn about that poor boy; you're only interested in your theories." Obviously Jung married the right woman.

From his book, *Marriage—Dead or Alive*, we may gather that Guggenbühl did, too. This is apparently the less-than-obvious secret of the "Guggenbühl style." When we encounter him at a professional meeting or a dinner party or hitching along the street with his knapsack on his back, those of us who are his juniors know immediately that "projections" are constellated in the space between us. We know they are our own and that Guggenbühl will treat them as "natural facts." We feel our vulnerability. Our power projection hides the other side of the picture from our view: Guggenbühl feels vulnerable. His own "projections" are out there, and he treats them as "natural facts" as well.

—John R. Haule

PREFACE
Deliver Us From Evil?

Most professions serve the health and well-being of humanity in one way or another. But the activities of the doctor, priest, teacher, psychotherapist, and social worker involve specialized and deliberate attempts to help the unfortunate, the ill, those who have somehow lost their way. In the following chapters I should like to describe how and why the members of these "ministering professions" can also do the greatest damage—harm caused directly by their very desire to help.

I work as a medical psychotherapist. In preparing psychiatric reports, I come into regular contact with social workers and often feel myself to be one of them. Many of my patients are teachers and clergymen. While writing this book, I was intent on seeing the beam in my own eye and not only the mote in the other person's. That is why I have concentrated chiefly on the power problems of the doctor and psychotherapist. However, to introduce the subject of destructiveness in the ministering professions, I have also explored some of the psychological background of social work and have touched briefly on the activities of clergymen and teachers.

Only in writing of doctors and psychotherapists, however, have I tried to explore in detail the possibility of overcoming the fundamental problems of their professions. It is my own house that I would like to set in order, leaving my neighbors to tend to theirs. But power problems and their mastery are similar in all the ministering professions, although each has its specific characteristics. This small book is therefore addressed not only to doctors and psychotherapists but also to social workers, teachers, and the clergy. For this reason I have tried to use a minimum of psychological terms which are not generally familiar. Wherever I have had to deviate from this practice, I have added a brief explanation of the specialized term. It is my hope that a member of a non-medical ministering profession will try to deal more deeply with the basic, personal problems found in his own field and to indicate possible solutions.

Literary references are practically absent from this book. My chief aim is to rouse the reader not to read still more, but rather to turn inward and examine himself. I have also refrained from trying to prove my assertions by citing experiments, statistics, and quotations from other authors. I hope to stimulate by presenting my experiences and those of my colleagues and co-workers. I am not necessarily interested in proving myself right.

The following pages contain frequent use of the words analysis, psychotherapy, analyst, and psychotherapist. To prevent misunderstanding, by psychotherapy I mean, quite generally, treatment dealing with the psyche. This ranges from psychological counselling lasting a few hours, up to an extended analysis of perhaps several hundred hours during which the most profound depths of the unconscious are explored and such phenomena as transference, countertransference, and the relation between analyst and analysand are discussed in detail. The analyst thus engages in a specialized form of psychotherapy. The power problems confronting the analyst and the general psychotherapist are basically the same. It is therefore unimportant for the reader whether, in any particular passage, we refer to psychotherapy or analysis.

A final prefatory thought: we of the ministering professions shall not be delivered from evil. But we can learn to deal with it.

CHAPTER ONE
Social Work and Inquisition

In welfare work, action must often be taken against the client's will, since he is not always capable of recognizing what is good for him. Under certain circumstances the social worker has legal means to execute such measures on the basis of his own judgment—and social workers find it highly regrettable when such means are lacking. For example, children who are severely maltreated and neglected by their parents can be taken out of their hands. Very often, however, though it is perfectly clear to the authorities that a child is growing up in unfavorable conditions, there are no legal grounds for stepping in. Only later, when the child is older, and perhaps comes into conflict with the law as a delinquent, is there a chance to take the necessary steps against the will of both child and parents. Many people involved in social work lament the fact that action often can be taken only when it is too late; they complain bitterly that it is so difficult to take children from their parents in their own best interests.

It is even more difficult to take enforced measures against adults. In Switzerland, however, a person who has put himself or his family in danger of a state of distress or destitution through squandering, alcoholism, depravity, or mismanagement of financial assets may be placed under guardianship.

According to the laws of Switzerland and most other countries, it is not always possible for a social worker to step in where and when he deems it necessary, but there are many situations in which measures may be taken against parents with regard to their children. An adult who has been placed under guardianship, for example, is not free to act contrary to the dictates of the social worker in charge. And youngsters under eighteen who commit even the slightest infringement of the law may be raised and educated until they are twenty-two years old according to the decree of the competent authorities.

Acting against the will of a client demands conviction. One must be certain that one's own ideas are right. The following case may illustrate this point. A girl of seventeen, let us call her Anna, lived with her twice-divorced mother. Following the mother's second divorce, the girl was placed under guardianship (as a result of complaints lodged by some people close to the family). It seemed that an unhealthy dependency existed between mother and daughter; the girl's every wish was granted. After completing school she took a succession of casual jobs and finally stopped working altogether. Although the mother complained of her daughter's behavior, she appeared to support her inactivity, obviously not wanting her to grow up and become independent. The social worker who meticulously investigated the case reached the conclusion, together with a psychiatrist, that mother and daughter should be separated. The girl's mental health was at stake. That both mother and daughter passionately resisted a separation could not be permitted to matter.

Even after the separation, it proved impossible to arouse the girl's interest in work. Everything seemed to indicate that she preferred letting men provide for her. To prevent her slipping into prostitution, her guardianship was prolonged after she reached the age of twenty.

SOCIAL WORK AND INQUISITION

The officials connected with the case agreed that it had been handled correctly in every respect. On what was this certitude based? It must not be forgotten that measures had been taken against the will of the individuals involved.

The social worker's activities are based on a philosophy originating in the Enlightenment, which assumes that people can and should be reasonable and socially adapted, that life's fulfillment consists in developing somewhat "normally" and happily within the limits of one's potential An infant, cared for by a loving mother, should develop into a satisfied child, and a responsible father should make it possible for the child to enjoy a lively and healthy youth in a more or less secure material framework. Following a happy period in school, the youngster should gradually detach himself from his parents, take up a profession, and as an un-neurotic, balanced, socially adjusted individual, find a mate with whom he will in turn have children whom he, as a contented father, will guide to maturity. When his children are grown and start their own families, he will experience the joys of grandfatherhood.

The goal of all our efforts, according to this basic philosophy, is to create healthy, socially adjusted people, happy in their interpersonal relations. Neurotic development, social maladjustment, eccentricity, and peculiar family relationships must be avoided and combated. When a person does not turn out happy and normal in these terms, it is presumed that something went wrong in early childhood, in his upbringing. If "properly" cared for—so it is assumed—most children will become well-balanced, happy adults. Care must be taken that development proceeds according to these accepted concepts, with or without the individual's assent.

At first glance it seems unquestionably correct that such a philosophy, which I have presented in a somewhat simplified form, should be the cornerstone of our actions. But the philosophy of "normalcy and social adjustment" did not always enjoy its present dominance. The early and medieval Christians, for example, held very different views. Their primary goal was not to raise healthy, un-neurotic, socially adjusted people, but to save their souls and help others to attain the Kingdom of Heaven. Concepts such as emotionally healthy or sick, socially adjusted or maladjusted, interpersonal relations, independence from parents, etc., played only a subsidiary role—or none at all. The way in which a Christian, until the Middle Ages, sought his soul's salvation would be considered by us today partly as neurotic and socially maladjusted. The leading models were the Saints, people who feared nothing in their efforts to approach God in their own way. There were, for example, the so-called Stylites or Pillar-saints, pious Christians of the Middle East who tried to serve God by spending the greater part of their lives sitting or standing on a pillar. They, as well as men of God who lived as hermits in the desert, were certainly not well-adjusted or socially integrated. Those saints who distributed all their worldly goods to the poor and spent their own lives as beggars would, according to §Paragraph 370 of the Swiss Civil Code, have to be placed under guardianship for putting themselves in danger of a state of distress or destitution. In terms of our philosophy of normalcy and adjustment, the ascetics who fasted and mortified themselves appear at best as unfortunate eccentrics, and at worst as mentally ill people in need of treatment.

When Christianity established itself in its medieval form, there were many who did not hold with the predominant views. Values other than the salvation of the soul in the

Christian sense were meaningful to them—which often proved to be a fatal attitude. At certain times and under certain circumstances, those who deviated in this manner, or advocated a different value hierarchy, were persecuted, martyred, and killed by the Church. Today the word "Inquisition" has an ominous ring. But the Christian Inquisitors were able to justify their deeds with absolute conviction and were considered, by themselves and their society, as well-meaning men. Leading Christians were absolutely certain that their views on the soul's salvation were the only correct ones. In this sense the Inquisitors had a twofold task: on the one hand they had to protect the general public from dangerous heresies which represented the gravest danger to men's souls, and on the other hand, they had to protect the heretics from their own imminent damnation. Through the shock of imprisonment and torture, they had to be made to see that their souls were in need of saving. The danger to society was eliminated by burning at the stake. If, when faced with the flames, a relapsed heretic admitted the error of his ways, he was burned anyway to save him from further relapses—but he was granted the mercy of being strangled beforehand. Thus the primary task of the Inquisition was not to persecute, torture, and kill; its lofty aim was to protect and help humanity in general and the individual in particular. And the Inquisitors believed that all possible means were considered justified in promulgating official doctrine which was the only right one.

Now it naturally cannot be maintained that today's social welfare endeavors are directly descended from the medieval Inquisition; there is no torture and no burning in social work. But there are certain obvious parallels. An attempt is made to combat unhealthy family situations, to

5

correct unsatisfactory social structures, to adjust the maladjusted—in brief, we try to enforce that which we consider "right" for people. And we often do this even when our help is rejected by those concerned. In our own way we frequently force a certain view of life upon others whether they agree to it or not. We do not choose to acknowledge a right to sickness, neurosis, unhealthy familial relations, social degeneracy, and eccentricity. The parallels between the Inquisition and modern social work should not be taken too literally. My point is that disposing of our fellow man against his will, even when this appears to us as the only proper course, can be highly problematical. We can never know wherein lies the real meaning of an individual human life. The goal of individual and collective actions is always seen somewhat differently by other people at other times. Our present values are not the only or final ones. Two hundred years from now they may already be regarded as primitive and ridiculous. Today there are movements within our Western society that despise and fight against the values of normalcy and social adjustment. The Hippies, and all their variations and subgroups, are one example. The long-haired wanderers who make pilgrimages from Europe to India, getting by on occasional work, begging, and finding their happiness in smoking hashish do not see social normalcy as the goal of life.

Awareness of the questionableness of our value systems should make us cautious about forcing those values on others. The Inquisitors had too few scruples in this regard. In retrospect, we now feel that it would have been better if they had gone more deeply into the motives behind their actions. In studying the Inquisition today, we can hardly avoid the suspicion that the psychological drives motivating those holy crusaders were not as pure as they pretended to themselves and the world; it seems to me that an unconscious cruelty and power drive was involved. ·

For many of us, the medieval Inquisition represents the epitome of officially sanctioned, sadistic lust for power. When, in modern social work, we sometimes force on an individual things which he himself rejects, our motives are surely better. Or perhaps not always? In my years of analytical work with social workers, I have noticed time and again that whenever something must be imposed by force, the conscious and unconscious motives of those involved are many-faceted. An uncanny lust for power lurks in the background; dreams and fantasies show motives which consciousness prefers to ignore. One welfare worker, for instance, dreamed that while driving his car, he ran over a person on whom, in waking life, he had imposed certain things. In his dream he was afraid lest it be discovered that he had done so intentionally. And even the emotions openly expressed during psychotherapy did not always indicate a pure desire to help.

"As I sat facing her, and she constantly contradicted me, I felt a desire to finally show her who was boss. I had a triumphant feeling that she did not realize how little she could do against my opposition." Such statements from social workers often accurately describe the emotional situation. Quite frequently, the issue at stake appears to be not the welfare of the protected but the power of the protector. The imposition of a carefully justified measure against the will of the person concerned often gives rise to a deep sense of satisfaction in the case worker—the same kind of satisfaction felt by a schoolboy who has thoroughly beaten up another, proven himself the stronger, and thinks: "That will show him! He'd better not fool around with me."

Another interesting psychological phenomenon has struck me. The greater the contamination by dark motives, the more the case worker seems to cling to his alleged "objectivity." In such cases the discussion of the actions to be taken in a case become blatantly dogmatic, as if there could be only one correct solution to the problem. An intelligent social worker who was analyzing with me once said: "Whenever I manage to prove to my colleagues that a particular enforced measure is as absolutely right as two-plus-two-make-four, I have unpleasant dreams at night, and opinions other than my own begin to seem to me like personal attacks."

All those active in the social professions, who work "to help humanity," have highly ambiguous psychological motives for their actions. In his own consciousness and to the world at large, the social worker feels obliged to regard the desire to help as his prime motivation. But in the depths of his soul the opposite is simultaneously constellated—not the desire to help but lust for power and joy in depotentiating the "client."

Particularly when a case worker is forced to operate against the will of the person concerned, careful analysis of the depths of the unconscious reveals the power drive as an important factor. In general the power drive is given free rein when it can appear under the cloak of objective and moral rectitude. People are the most cruel when they can use cruelty to enforce the "good." In daily life we often suffer pangs of conscience when we permit ourselves to be excessively motivated by the power drive. But these guilt feelings completely disappear from consciousness when our actions, while unconsciously motivated by a lust for power, can be consciously justified by that which is allegedly right and good.

SOCIAL WORK AND INQUISITION

The problem of the "power shadow" is therefore of paramount importance for the social worker who is sometimes obliged to make important decisions against the will of the people involved. But at this point I should like to avoid certain misunderstandings: No one can act out of exclusively pure motives. Even the noblest deeds are based on pure and impure, light and dark motivations. Because of this, many people and their actions are unjustly ridiculed or compromised. A generous philanthropist is almost always motivated, among other things, by the desire to be respected and honored for his generosity. His philanthropy is in no way less valuable for that. Similarly, a social worker strongly prompted by power motives may nevertheless make decisions helpful to his client. But there is a great danger that the more the case worker pretends to himself that he is operating only from selfless motives, the more influential his power shadow will become until it finally betrays him into making some very questionable decisions.

In Switzerland there are those who advocate an extension of the Juvenile Penal Code beyond the age of twenty. We might question whether this, like many similar views, is not an expression of the social worker's power shadow (which is naturally also to be found in related professions, such as public prosecutor, attorney for juvenile delinquents, etc.). The Juvenile Penal Code protects a youthful lawbreaker from having a purely formalized penalty imposed on him and makes it possible to reeducate or rehabilitate him. But—and this is unavoidable—it at the same time subjects him to the more or less arbitrary will of the authorities. Were the Juvenile Penal Code to be extended to cover people up to the age of twenty-five, for example, this would mean in effect that a young man of twenty-two who

9

commits a minor infraction of the law would not merely have to pay for his crime, but that he could be forced to accept a rehabilitation program which would be longer and harder than the punishment dictated by the normal penal code for adults. Instead of being subjected to a penalty specified by law, he would find himself at the pedagogical mercies of the authorities, who would presumably try to compel him through reeducation to change.

Here we might give let our imaginations go. Many social workers and some interested jurists have proposed that the general penal code be reformed to eliminate specific penalties entirely, leaving only educative measures. A lawbreaker would no longer be punished but instead helped through re- education to become a socially adjusted individual. This would mean that any citizen guilty of violating the law could be examined concerning his character and social attitudes; were it discovered that his character did not meet the standards and values of his examiners, he could be forcibly educated to an inner change. To formulate the situation more pointedly: under certain circumstances, violation of a parking regulation could lead to several years of rehabilitation. The social worker charged with recommending or executing such measures would find himself with unprecedented power. This is why I earlier posed the question of whether such reform proposals might not be partly the expression of a widespread power shadow. I am repeatedly impressed by the difficulty dedicated social workers have in accepting the fact that parental rights are strongly protected. In Switzerland, even when the authorities believe it self-evident that certain children are being badly raised by their parents and in all probability will have serious difficulty in later life, they are powerless to intervene unless the case is one of crass neglect or maltreatment. "But that's absolute nonsense," maintain many social workers. "It should be possible to stop the parents before they ruin the children!"

Here again the question arises of whether, behind this forceful demand for a chance to intervene, there may not lurk the social worker's power shadow. One case worker tried very hard to take a child away from what were, in her opinion, completely unfit parents; she failed for lack of legal grounds. In telling me of this, she said with admirable candor: "The main thing I feel now is fury and hatred for those parents. I'd really like to show them a thing or two!" Her frustration at not having proven herself stronger than the parents was far greater than her regret at not having succeeded in helping the child.

To illustrate this even more clearly, I want to return to the case of Anna cited earlier. A thorough examination of our own motives was urgently needed at that time. Perhaps it was not so certain that anything beneficial could be accomplished by taking the daughter from her mother. The two of them admittedly had an unhealthy relationship. But it was doubtful whether our forcible interference did more good than harm. As I have already tried to indicate, our ideas of health and normalcy may not represent the ultimate wisdom. Might the daughter not also have been able to lead a meaningful life while bound to her mother? Were we more capable than both mother and daughter, who resisted the separation, of seeing what constituted a "meaningful" way of life? Did we really want to help them? Or were we the victims of our own unconscious power drives? I would even go further. Why were we so certain that it was absolutely the proper thing to prolong the girl's guardianship beyond her twentieth birthday in order to save her from prostitution? Could we really have known that placing her in such a position would not do great harm? In fact, the extended guardianship did not actually change the girl's behavior at all nor did one year in a reformatory. One often hears the complaint voiced by social workers that people only turn to the authorities when they are at the end of their rope. Then if they are given counselling, they listen carefully and promptly do the opposite of what they have been advised, turning up again only when their actions have resulted in calamity. Social workers become furious at such behavior and regret that there are not more ways of enforcing their advice. But is this anger and regret really an expression of social eros, or merely of a disappointed bid for power? True eros does not involve wanting to impose our own plan, or own ideas, on others.

The presence of a power problem in the field of social work is also indirectly confirmed by the following: the basic structure of most professions is reflected in public opinion about it. There are definite collective views on the professional character of social workers, doctors, clergymen, lawyers, politicians, etc. The collective image is usually a double one, with a light and a dark side. The negative collective image of a particular profession is generally more unitary and standardized than the positive image. Clergymen are represented as hypocrites, teachers as childish and unworldly, physicians as quacks, and so on. Naturally such positive and negative images must be regarded partly as prejudices. But if these collective ideas are carefully examined, they often prove to be partially valid, if distorted, reflections of the professions concerned.

The problem of the power shadow plays a prominent role in the negative collective image of the social worker. He appears in it as someone who interferes whenever possible, forcing his will on people without really understanding what is going on, trying to bring everything into line according to narrow, moralistic, bourgeois standards. He is prompted to do this by a delight in power, and is insulting and malicious when his power is not acknowledged.

Concretized in a situation, this "negative mythology" of the social worker might look something like this. At ten in the morning the social worker knocks at the door of an apartment. He enters, snoops around, and observes that the beds are unmade and last night's dishes unwashed. The lady of the house is not yet dressed. Clad only in a bathrobe, she is just beginning her daily chores. On the basis of this visit, the social worker concludes that the family is unfit to keep its foster child. The child, passionately loved by its adoptive parents, is taken away in order to be placed in a proper, bourgeois household. The social worker's opinion is negative not only because of the disorder she found there, but also because the woman of the house rejected her interference and at first was even disinclined to let him into the apartment.

At this point the objection might be raised that what I have said thus far may perhaps apply to the old fashioned, traditional welfare worker, who may indeed have had a great power shadow, but that the problem is far less acute in modern social work. Today's enlightened case worker is psychologically trained, tries to understand and help people in accord with psychological knowledge. His basic attitudes are often hardly different from those of a psychotherapist. It has been my experience, however, that a knowledge of psychology may refine the power problem but in no way does it eliminate it. In fact a knowledge of psychology can to a large extent be pressed into the service of the power shadow for it can create a situation in which the client is even robbed of the mastery of his own soul.

Not only the client's social and financial situation, but even his personal psychology has become transparent to and manipulatable by the case worker. And when psychological tests are added to the social worker's battery of tools, the unfortunate client is totally helpless. He can only dimly perceive that his soul has been X-rayed and that he has indirectly revealed his innermost being to those who are supposed to help him. The social worker then becomes able to tell a mother who insists that she loves her child, that in reality she is unrelated to him. He can tell a youngster desperately resisting years of rehabilitation that he actually is glad to have some limits imposed upon him. The individual concerned has nothing more to say because the social worker's X-ray vision has seen through him.

This already touches on the shadow problems of another profession, that of psychotherapist, which is actually the focal point of this book. We shall turn to it in the next chapter. Before doing so, however, I want to add a few thoughts on a less negative note.

People take up the difficult and responsible profession of social worker for a variety of psychological reasons which differ with each individual. Although chance occurrences also play their part, there are certain motivations common to social workers which have prompted their choice of profession. I am not speaking here of those who practice their profession in a cynical spirit, purely as a means of earning a living. For such people, at any rate, the problem of the power shadow is not especially acute. It is primarily the assiduous, enthusiastic social workers, truly dedicated, who repeatedly fall victim to the power shadow. The cynical and indifferent individual simply does his job formally and correctly and is deeply touched by neither the positive nor the negative aspects of his work.

SOCIAL WORK AND INQUISITION

What drives a man to concern himself with the dark side of social life? What makes it possible for him to deal each day with unhappy, unfortunate, maladjusted people? What fascinates him about this dismal side of life? He must, in the final analysis, be a special sort of person. The average "healthy" individual prefers to ignore and forget the misfortunes and sufferings of his fellow man whenever he is not directly concerned, or perhaps to encounter them now and again at a comfortable distance in the newspaper or on television. Only a relative few care to be confronted daily with the concerns of others; most people have enough of their own. Merely to say that social workers are people blessed with a greater than normal love of their fellows does not get us anywhere, since it is not true. Nor are all social workers believing Christians who hold that love of one's neighbor, expressed by helping the unfortunate, is God's greatest commandment. At the same time, we must not regard the desire to help as only a rationalization of the shadow side of the profession—of the power drive. It is, of course, tempting to reduce something admirable to something much less admirable. There are many psychological works set out to show how an expression of eros, for example, is in fact merely the sublimation of some base instinct. In this view the painter is a frustrated infantile smearer, the teacher a repressed child-seducer, the psychotherapist a voyeur, etc.

It must be a special breed of person who chooses as his life's work the daily confrontation with some of humanity's most fundamental polarities: adjustment—maladjustment, social success—social failure, mental health—mental sickness. Certainly, members of the ministering professions are more fascinated by such polarities than are other people.

Chapter Two
Psychotherapist:
Charlatan and False Prophet

Psychotherapy in its present form is relatively young. The model upon which the therapist bases his activities is derived from various other professions and cannot be understood except in relation to more ancient arts. Like it or not, psychotherapy is related to medicine. The professional and ethical models which guide the physician are in part those of the psychotherapist as well, and the dark sides of the analyst are to a certain extent linked to the medical character of his work.

The physician undertakes to help the sick and the suffering. The Hippocratic Oath reads in part: "The regimen I adopt shall be for the benefit of my patients according to my ability and judgment, and not for their hurt or for any wrong. Whatsoever house I enter, there will I go for the benefit of the sick, refraining from all wrongdoing or corruption. I shall regard my life and my Art as sacred." In its general outlines, this lofty conception of the doctor is familiar to many people of the Western world.

The dark sides of a physician's activities are not to be found in the Hippocratic Oath. They were ably caricatured in *Dr. Knock,* a play by Jules Romain. Dr. Knock has no wish to heal others selflessly. He uses his medical knowledge for his personal advantage, not even hesitating to turn healthy people into sick ones. His philosophy is, "There are no healthy people, only sick people who don't know they are ill." Dr. Knock is a charlatan. By this term I do not

mean someone who uses unorthodox or officially unac-
cepted methods to help the ailing, but rather those doctors
who at best fool their patients and themselves, or at worst,
their patients alone. They help themselves, financially and
in terms of prestige, more than they do the sick people
seeking their aid. Understood in this sense, the activities of
a charlatan may in any particular case be beneficial, harmful, or entirely neutral.

Charlatanism is a form of shadow which accompanies
the physician everywhere. It is one of his dark brothers. As
such it may live in him or outside of him. Some doctors see
this shadow in the person of the obscure quack or "nature
healer." But most physicians frequently fall victim to the
charlatan shadow in the course of their professional activities. Patients exert considerable pressure on the doctor to
betray the Hippocratic model and act instead as a Dr. Knock.
All the countless complaints of indeterminate origin with
which the general practitioner must deal every day, and for
which no genuine therapy has yet been found—chronic
fatigue, certain pains of the back and joints, vague heart
and stomach disorders, chronic headache, etc.—are commonly treated by pseudo-scientific means. By not pointing
out the emotional components to those patients whose
bodily complaints are largely psychic in origin, the average
physician encourages his patients to emphasize even more
the somatic aspects of their emotional problems. If the
symptoms improve, he is the great healer. If they deterio-
rate, it is obvious that the patient has failed to carry out his
instructions.

A lovely historical example of the operation of this charlatan shadow, dating from the eleventh century, may be
found in the seriously-intended hints offered by
Archimatheus of Salerno who wrote: "To the patient prom-

ise a cure, and to the members of his family give warning of grave illness. If the patient fails to recover, it will be said that you foresaw his death; if he is cured, your renown will grow." But the psychotherapist draws his models only partly from the field of medicine. The other vocation which influences his ideals is that of the priest.

The image of the man of God has undergone many changes in the course of history and is not the same among all religions. The important image for our purposes is that of the religious leader of the Judeo-Christian tradition. He is supposed to be a man who, at least now and again, is in contact with God. Not all clergymen are expected, like the Old Testament prophets, to receive their vocation directly from the Deity, but they are expected to sincerely try to act on God's behalf and in accordance with His will.

The dark side of this noble image of the man of God is the lying hypocrite, the man who preaches not because he believes but in order to gain influence and power. As in the case of the doctor and his patients, so with the clergyman it is frequently the members of his congregation who involuntarily activate his dark brother. They exert considerable pressure on him to play the hypocrite. Doubt is the companion of faith. But no one wants to hear doubt expressed by a clergyman; we all have doubts enough of our own. Thus the priest often has no alternative but to be the hypocrite now and again, to hide his own doubts, and to mask a momentary inner emptiness with high flown words. If his character is weak, this can become a habitual stance.

A man of God, in the ideal, sense must bear witness to his faith by his actions. He cannot prove what he preaches. He is expected to provide by his behavior a foundation for the faith which he represents. And this opens the door to another of the clergyman's dark brothers—the one who wishes to present himself to the world (and to himself) as better than he really is.

The shadow of the false prophet accompanies the clergyman all his life. Sometimes it appears externally, as the preacher of some obscure sect or as a colleague grown popular through demagoguery; at other times it rises up inside himself. Many modern clergymen, however, have a strong fear of this hypocritical, false prophet shadow. They refuse to be characterized as "men of God" through inner or outer traits. They deliver their sermons dressed in everyday clothes, in an attitude of casual social converse.

We analysts deal often with disturbances of health for which, in terms of both treatment and possible cure, accepted controls of an experimental nature are hardly possible—neurosis and psychosis—therefore it is virtually impossible to accumulate statistics on successful treatment of them. What constitutes improvement? What deterioration? Should social adjustment serve as a criterion? The ability to work? The increase and intensification, or decrease and amelioration of neurotic symptoms? The patient's subjective feelings? Progress in psychological development, in the individuation process, in contact with the unconscious? Even the criteria is uncertain, as opposed to a straightforward somatic complaint where a restoration of functioning provides an unequivocal yardstick for the success of treatment. In the case of emotional problems including psychosomatic ailments, generally, whatever criteria is used provides unsatisfactory results. Even with large statistical samplings, it is difficult to make qualitative judgements about the course of the disturbances involved, whether one treats them with intensive psychotherapy, with tranquillizers, or with nothing at all. The nearness or remoteness from the "self," from the "meaning of life," a better or worse contact with the unconscious, may be criteria which can indicate the success of psychotherapy. But how are such factors to be measured and statistically investigated?

Anyone can register a success in treatment if he happens to be on hand at the right moment, sticks with a patient long enough, and is fortunate to stumble on someone looking for help whose condition would have improved anyway in terms of one or more of the criteria we have enumerated. The charlatan shadow of the analyst's medically oriented aspect can thus operate more or less freely. Moreover, such terms as sick and healthy, in need of treatment or not, are, in general, far more difficult to apply to a person's emotional state than to his physical condition. The psychic development of every individual is highly complex, and each of us is somewhat neurotic. A psychotherapist operating like Dr. Knock could prove quite easily to nearly anyone that a long analysis is unavoidable. The matter can be pushed so far that anyone who has never been in analysis feels himself somehow sick or at least not completely developed psychologically.

The analyst's shadow is further enlarged by the traits which the psychotherapist shares with the clergyman. We analysts, regardless of which school of psychology we subscribe to, advocate no specific faith or organized religion, but like clergymen, we often do stand for a certain basic attitude of life. We represent no philosophy, but indeed a psychology to which we adhere out of conviction, since in our lives and in our own analyses we have had experiences which persuaded and formed us in terms of that psychology. The Jungian analyst, for instance, has been deeply shaken by the encounter with the irrational and the unconscious. There are few psychological insights, however, which can be statistically proven in the empirical sense. They can only be confirmed by the sincere, honest testimony of other seekers. Our only proof is the experience of ourselves and others, since psychic reality cannot be grasped statistically or causally in the sense of the natural sciences. Here we find ourselves in a position similar to that of clergymen. But such utter reliance on the personal experience of oneself and others inevitably raises grave doubts. What if we and others like us have deceived ourselves? There are, after all, many other men of integrity, psychotherapists who advocate completely different schools of thought. Are they all deceiving themselves? Are they all blind? Or could the situation be as it is described, in Mary McCarthy's novel, *The Group*, by a psychiatrist who has decided to give up his profession to pursue research on the biochemistry of the brain: "That is why I am getting out of it (psychiatry); if you stay, you have your choice of becoming a cynic or a naive fraud." Are we capable of admitting these doubts to ourselves and the world around us? Or do we psychotherapists do with our doubts and fears what clergymen often do with theirs—suppress them and keep the lid on tight?

Again, like clergymen, we work with our souls, with our selves; methods, techniques, and apparatus are secondary. We, our honesty and genuineness, our personal contact with the unconscious and the irrational—these are our tools. There is pressure to represent these tools as better than they really are and thus to become the victim of our psychotherapeutic shadow.

There is still another parallel to priests: we analysts are often forced into a role of omniscience. We work with the unconscious, with dreams, and the psyche, realms in which the transcendental manifests itself—at least in the view of

many laymen and even many therapists. And so it is expected that we know more about ultimate matters than
does the common mortal. If we are weak, we eventually
come to believe ourselves that we are more deeply initi-
ated into life and death than are our fellow men. It is not
only the more noble images of medicine and the priesthood which converge in the analyst but their shadow aspects
as well—the charlatan and the false prophet.

The problem of the analyst's shadow is further intensified by something which is specific to him and not
necessarily linked to the basic models of other professions.
It is the fact that one of the psychotherapist's tasks is to
help his patients to become more conscious.

Just as a knowledge of God plays a central role in the
ideal model of the priest, and the selfless healer in the
image of the physician, a crucial position in the model of
the psychotherapist is taken by a figure which we might
term the maker of consciousness or "the bringer of the
light." But professional images always have a dark aspect
which represents the opposite of the bright ideal. The
analyst's professional shadow contains not only the charlatan and the false prophet, but also the counter pole to the
bringer of the light, a figure who lives completely in the
unconscious and strives for the opposite of the analyst's
conscious goals. We have a paradoxical situation in which
the analyst is more threatened by the unconscious than is
the non-analyst. The honest psychotherapist is shocked
from time to time by the realization that he has been operating completely from the unconscious in his work.

The analyst often receives no warning from his patient
when he is being unconsciously destructive, for the patient
is himself oriented toward the charlatan and false prophet
in the analyst and encourages these aspects. A therapist

often has the impression that his work is going splendidly, the deeper he falls into his own shadow. Just as the physician is forced into the role of charlatan by his patients, and the clergyman into that of false prophet by his congregation, the analyst is repeatedly pushed into these unconscious roles by his analysands.

An important objection might be voiced here. If he is professionally sincere, an analyst remains in contact with his own unconscious, carefully studying his dreams and any other statements the unconscious may make. One would think this would certainly prevent him from falling into the role of charlatan, false prophet, and unconsciously destructive analyst. But that is not the case. Like other people, we analysts often have a blind spot in regard to our shadow. We see it neither in our dreams nor in our actions. Frequently even our friends cannot see our shadow for a time, becoming as blind as we are ourselves, resulting in something resembling a *folie a deux*. In such cases enemies can be useful; we should study their statements with care.

There are a few rules which we use in interpreting the statements of the unconscious. But in the final analysis such interpretation is an art rather than a craft, and our own personal equation may repeatedly mislead us into overlooking something crucial. There is also the difficulty that statements from the unconscious, like those of the Delphic Oracle, are almost invariably ambivalent. And whether one chooses to understand the unconscious in one way or in another, depends on the ego. What happened to Croesus with the Oracle can happen to us as well; that is, we may interpret the unconscious in keeping with our ego-wishes and thus misunderstand it.

Anticipating some later remarks, I would like at this point to just touch on the question of what consequences may be drawn from the fact that we sometimes fall prey to our professional shadow.

We demand truthfulness from our patients. We help the patient in his sincere confrontation with the unconscious through our explanations, our dream interpretations, but above all by our own attitude and manner. By looking our own professional shadow in the eye, we show our analysands that the unpleasant sides of life must also be faced. As I have tried to indicate, an important role in our analytical work, and thus in our relations to our patients, is played by the shadow figures of the completely unconscious charlatan and false prophet. If a patient gets wind of this shadow, it is crucial for the further progress of therapy that we be capable of admitting to him our own backsliding into the unconscious and the professional shadow, no matter how painful such an admission may be. The patient, after all, must also face up to painful insights. By constantly trying to spot the workings of our psychotherapeutic shadow, to catch it red-handed, we help our patients in their own confrontations with the dark brother. If we fail to do this, all the patient learns from us is how to fool himself and the world, and the value of the analysis becomes highly questionable.

The problem of the professional shadow touches other fundamentals of psychotherapeutic activity. As analysts we constantly deal with severe suffering, with uncommon and tragic destinies. Often what is required of us is to help a troubled person to understand himself as far as possible, not only to take up contact with the unconscious but also simply to bear the tragic aspects of life in all their incomprehensibility. In order to help an ailing person in a tragic life situation—in a situation which remains tragic even if contact with the unconscious improves—we must also be able to face our own tragic situation, the tragedy that, the more we try to be good psychotherapists and to help our patients to broader consciousness, the more we repeatedly slip into the opposite of our bright professional ideal.

In a certain sense, the fate of every person who is striving for something—and our patients are generally such people—has a distinctly tragic side to it. The opposite of what one wants to attain or avoid is repeatedly being constellated. This is true in the collective and in the individual. The French Revolution sought to free men and brought the Napoleonic tyranny. In the nineteenth century, many Swiss men interested in singing tried to promote it as an activity by founding male choirs. But in fact the existence of these male choruses completely destroyed singing as a popular pastime among the general populace, making it instead something which was done only within the organized framework of a choir under the direction of a conductor. Christianity, preaching peace and love, caused bloody Crusades, and the Crusaders, fired by a desire to conquer the Holy Land, first tried to exterminate the Jews of Europe. C. G. Jung repeatedly pointed out that, whenever a bright psychic content becomes lodged in consciousness, its opposite is constellated in the unconscious and tries to do harm from that vantage point. The physician becomes a charlatan precisely because he wants to heal as many people as possible; the clergyman becomes a hypocrite and false prophet precisely because he wants to bring people to the true faith, and the psychotherapist becomes an unconscious charlatan and false prophet although he works day and night on becoming more conscious.

My statements thus far may seem rather gloomy, like those of a Calvinist preacher or a theologian of ancient

Iceland—if there had been theologians in those days. Odin does what he can, although he knows full well that the roots of the world ash tree, Iggdrasil, are being slowly but surely destroyed by a serpent.

But the existence of the psychotherapist's shadow also has aspects which are somewhat less tragic. The actions of a therapist operating from the shadow are not always negative. Charlatans often do more to ameliorate suffering than respectable, earnest physicians. And a therapist temporarily falling into the unconscious and operating completely from the shadow side, can by his external sureness and definiteness help many patients, at least temporarily, by taking the edge off their more acute suffering.

One of my analysands once had the following dream: in a newspaper he saw a caricature of me, done in the Daumier style, and under it were the words, "Unfortunately our colleague Dr. A. G.-C. has misused the noble art of medicine, as a charlatan, to his own advantage." At the time I did not think the dream actually referred to me but interpreted it as the expression of a resistance based on collective prejudices against psychology, psychotherapy, and the unconscious. I rejected the criticism leveled at me, the portrait of my professional shadow as a caricature *a la* Daumier and took it as a subjective problem of the patient. In the course of the analysis we subsequently returned to this dream and saw quite clearly that it referred to my own professional shadow problem. But my patient also said he was glad that we had failed to understand the dream completely when it first came up. The certainty with which I had referred the dream back to him, though it was based on my unconsciousness, had a calming effect on him. At that time, he said, he could not have borne the strain of having to deal with my shadow as well as his own.

I could well imagine a critical reaction to the remarks I have made so far in this chapter. Are they not perhaps destructive? Why should we try at all to become more conscious, if we are doomed to fall back again and again into the most unpleasant kinds of unconsciousness? Why not "live and let live," cheerfully unconscious, and simply try to help our patients with medication? For those who are concerned with it professionally, the effort to become more conscious appears condemned to tragic failure. It is perhaps with good reason that certain East Asian religions try to cut loose completely from the demands and strivings of the ego, to free the individual from earthly concerns so that one can approach Nirvana. All the ego's efforts, no matter how earnestly intended, only do harm in the long run.

But Europeans cannot and will not renounce the ego. They must take its strivings and its goals seriously. The self—the meaningful and purposive center of the psyche according to Jung—can in general only appear if the ego is not brushed aside and killed off as insignificant, but runs aground in tragic involvement.

Oedipus tried desperately to live and act according to the will of the gods—that is, the unconscious. Apollo informed him, by means of the Oracle, that he would kill his father and marry his mother. To avoid this, young Oedipus left his father Polybos and his mother Merope, unaware that they were his adoptive rather than his real parents, since they had never told him about his true lineage. But his deliberate attempt to avoid the horrible and cursed deeds predicted for him led to the opposite. At the end of the tragedy, self-condemned, he describes himself as, "the most cursed of men, hated by all the gods." Having blinded himself he cries: "Nothing is left for sight. Nor anything to love. Nor shall the sound of greetings any more fall pleasant on my ear. Away! Out of the land, away! Banishment, banishment!"

But it is precisely in this tragic breakdown of Oedipal ego that the self, the divine spark in man, begins to shine through. As in every tragedy, one senses here a meaning which is no longer ego-oriented. Something similar is felt by every analyst—and with him, by his patients—who tries to be related to the unconscious, to live as consciously as possible, and to practice his profession in these terms. And in doing so he must increasingly fall into his own shadow and time and again play the charlatan and false prophet to his patients.

Up to now my remarks about the psychotherapist's dark brother have been perhaps too general. In the next chapter we will deal more closely with the charlatan, the false prophet, and other dark figures and see in practical terms what happens when the psychotherapist falls into the unconscious.

CHAPTER THREE
The Initial Contact Between Analyst and Analysand

As a rule an analyst's unconsciousness does not relate primarily to his own neurotic traits. In the course of their training analysis and their own analytical work, serious therapists have learned not to draw their patients into their own neurotic mechanisms.

But difficulties arise for the analyst out of his own desire to help. He wants to serve his patients, to aid them in their neurotic suffering, to try to stimulate greater consciousness in them. To the best of his knowledge and ability, he wants to help his patients selflessly, without which the opposite pole in the unconscious conjures up the charlatan; the analyst who works not for his patients but for himself. This is part of the psychological phenomenon which Jung often termed the "shadow." This term should not be confused with the term unconscious per se. By shadow Jung means the reverse side of personal or collective ideals. In this sense, the shadow is always somewhat destructive, operating negatively on the positive ideals taken up by the collective or the individual. The existence of the shadow is highly unpleasant and painful to the ego, whose goals are precisely the opposite. Conscience or the superego is formed by the immediate or more general environment in terms of existing ideals. The ego constantly tries to fulfill the demands of the superego or at least get by with compromises. The fact that there is a perpetual split between conscious values and the power of the shadow, which would like to destroy those values, creates dynamic tension but also painful insecurity. Every analysand must at times deal intensively with his own shadow, with all the demons operating within him, perhaps without his conscious knowledge.

Now let us turn concretely to the psychotherapist's shadow and describe some of its attributes. Shadow aspects may be constellated in the very first encounter between the therapist and patient. When the two meet for the first time, they both have conscious intentions. The patient wishes to be freed from his suffering, from neurotic symptoms such as compulsions, phobias, impotence, frigidity, depressive moods, psychosomatic ailments. Patients often seek help with life's general difficulties, problems in marriage, or with children, etc. Like the organically ill patient who turns to a physician, the psychotherapeutic patient wants release from his suffering and sickness. At least, that is how it seems on the psychic surface. The deeper expectations are often quite different. Unconsciously, at least in part, the patient often hopes to find a redeemer who will free him of all his problems and perhaps even awaken superhuman capacities in him. An intelligent patient of mine, who in addition to her severe neurosis also suffered from frequent colds, confessed to me a few months after the start of the analysis that she had hoped through psychotherapy to become immune against all physical illness. Her constant sniffles were a test; at the start of the therapy she had fantasized that, if her colds would disappear, she would gradually become able to use her psychic powers to ward off all physical ailments. The patient often looks to the psychotherapist not only for effective support in a fight against neurosis, but also for access to secret knowledge which will find a solution to al' of life's problems.

Husbands or wives often hope at the start of therapy to be given the tools with which to see through their marriage partners and bring them to complete submission. I recall one woman who came for treatment because of repeated neurotic outbreaks and chronic headache. During our second hour she declared that she was so happy to begin getting a glimmer of insight into the reasons for her suffering, because she would soon be able to show her husband how unfair he was and how badly he treated her.

At the start of therapy, the relation between therapist and patient is often like that of the sorcerer and his apprentice. And the patient's sorcerer and apprentice fantasies have a powerful effect on the therapist in whose unconscious the figure of the magician or savior begins to be constellated. The therapist starts to think that in fact he is someone with supernatural powers, capable of working wonders with his magic.

The patient's expectation and hope of finding a powerful sorcerer also plays some part in the choice of analyst. The analyst, of course, finds it extremely difficult not to be affected by this magician projection. In fact often he even stimulates it in the patient by trying to stress his power and prestige. When the patient tells him of his troubles, the analyst lets it be seen that he already understands everything. Through the use of certain gestures, such as a sage nodding of the head and of pregnant remarks interjected among the patient's statements, the analyst creates an impression that, while he may not be prepared to communicate all his knowledge and profound thoughts, he has already plumbed the depths of his patient's soul. This claim to absolute mastery is also a part of the sorcerer's image. As a rule, sorcerers want to be omnipotent and are unwilling to tolerate any colleagues or competitors. The relationship among sorcerers is generally a power struggle, consisting of magic and counter-magic. Fascinated by this inner figure of the magician, the average analyst would like all those in need of help to turn exclusively to him. For sheer lack of time, he may graciously refer a case to some beginner now and again but will still try to keep all the threads in his own hands. Many an analyst works himself nearly to death and speaks with a certain pride of his long waiting list of would be patients. An inner claim to absolute power, the fantasy that he is the best and most powerful of sorcerers, makes it impossible for him willingly to send cases to colleagues of equal status, not merely students or beginners. The analyst does not believe, like Snow White's stepmother, that he is the "fairest in the land," but a devilish little sorcerer within him lays claim to being the only one in the country who really understands anything about analysis.

The game of sorcerer and apprentice is often played not only at the start of an analysis but right on to its end and even beyond. Training analyses in particular are subject to this danger. The trainee may remain an "apprentice" for the rest of his life, that is, an admirer and imitator of his training analyst. Or he may try to become a master sorcerer himself, which leads to bitter recriminations between old master and former apprentice; the younger analyst harbors deep resentments against his older colleague, while the latter feels himself betrayed. The two can no longer work together. A father projection which has not been withdrawn is often not enough to explain the friction which arises between a training analyst and his professionally matured trainees.

Before pursuing the phenomenon of the shadow on psychotherapy any further, a few general remarks are in order.

As we have seen, the shadows of therapist and patient affect one another and are often linked in a close relationship. We therefore cannot get proper hold of the therapist's shadow without also dealing with that of the patient. The professional shadow of the therapist who wishes to help his patients is the charlatan, the fraudulent healer who pursues his own interests. Parallel to this we find in a patient who comes for treatment in order to be healed or to promote his own psychic development, a psychic force which struggles mightily against the process of healing or development, an anti-therapeutic force. It is often described as "resistance." This inner resistance fighter is aggressive. It not only resists the progress of therapy but actively tries to destroy it. At the end of this book, we will try to comprehend this so-called resistance more deeply. For now we will simply note that the patient's resistance often forms an alliance with the therapist's charlatan shadow; that resistance and charlatan mutually constellate each other and sometimes, though not always, cannot be understood without taking this mutuality into account.

In many respects the initial situation in therapy is well suited to constellate the charlatan shadow. For instance it may prompt the analyst to accept, if possible, only prosperous and prominent people for treatment; people who can pay high fees and whose names bring prestige. This tendency is in turn encouraged by the fact that patients would like to boast of working with a prominent analyst.

The charlatan in the analyst also uses the trick of needlessly dramatizing a situation. A neurotic patient is seen as having "dangerous psychotic potential." The term "latent psychosis," often used by Jung, can easily be misused in this way. The danger of a psychotic breakdown can be blown up to make the analyst appear as a savior. This in turn satisfies a need in the kind of patient who would like to see himself passively rescued, in an interesting manner of course, from a seemingly hopeless situation. The situation is analogous to that of patients with physical ailments who greatly enjoy being able to say, "All the doctors had given up on me, but then I consulted Dr. Healem, and today I'm a healthy man."

At the start of treatment, the establishment of the fee plays some role. A certain charlatanism often shows up in the analyst's attitude here. It is remarkable how often psychotherapists find it necessary to emphasize that the fee is itself a therapeutic necessity for promoting the healing process. May this not be, among other things, a shadow statement? The fee, after all, is not "therapy;" it is there to permit the therapist to live in a manner appropriate to a man of his level of education and training. Here, too, we find a counterpart in the patient. He is often willing to pay a high fee because it gives him the impression that he is buying the analyst, who, as his employee, will save him the trouble of honestly examining himself. At the same time, he pretends to himself that, because he has chosen the most expensive analyst, he is certain to be helped.

CHAPTER FOUR
Relationship is Fantasy

Once an analysis has gotten under way and the psyches of therapist and patient have begun to affect one another, a fruitful field of operation is opened up for the charlatan shadow. But in order to see through all its dodges in this case, we must first describe more precisely the character and modes of the mutual psychic influence of patient and analyst. The terms transference and countertransference, which we will use here, are often applied with variable meanings.

First, let us examine transference and countertransference as compared to encounter or relationship. In transference, something is seen in another person which is really not there at all or perhaps only in latent or nascent form. As is commonly known, a patient may see in the analyst a father or brother, a lover, a son or daughter, and so on—that is, he may transfer onto the analyst the traits of those figures who have played a part in his life. Psychic structures of one's own may also be transferred onto one's partner; qualities are seen in the other which are actually problematical in oneself. The term transference is commonly used to describe these phenomena.

By way of contrast: in a relationship or a genuine encounter, the partner is seen for what he is. He is experienced, loved, or hated, as he really exists; the encounter is with another real person. Naturally, transference and relationship usually occur simultaneously; they cannot be strictly differentiated as phenomena in any given case. At best, transference becomes relationship. Many friendships begin as a transference and only develop into a genuine relationship later. In my opinion it is destructive to try, as psychologists often do, to explain every relationship in terms of projection and transference. The chief virtue of such a procedure may be to flatter the psychologist's ego, since he believes he has grasped one of the most mysterious of psychological phenomena—that of relationship—by applying the simple concepts of transference and projection.

The mystery of relationship can only be vaguely described; it cannot be clearly grasped with the intellect. It means, as I have already indicated, seeing the other as he is, or at least partly recognizing him as the person he is. It also means deriving pleasure or displeasure from the person realistically seen, enjoying being with him, or doing something with him, turning to him with interest, exchanging emotions, feelings, and thoughts. In other words, in a relationship the partner is only minimally violated by projections or transference. However in this context the dynamism of the psyche and of the individual is often overlooked. What is the other, the partner? He is never something static; he is life, development, past, present, and future. To comprehend another person means relating not only to his present but to his past and future.

Relationship always involves something creative. In using the word "creative," I mean the following: the human psyche is always full of new possibilities. It is constantly recreating itself, so to speak, and is perpetually being recreated. An individual's psychic potential is limited, of course, but it is highly varied and many faceted. When we meet someone, it is unrelated and uncreative to see him as a fixed image. To encounter a person creatively means to weave fantasies around him, to circle around his potential. Various images arise about the person and the potential relationship to him. Such creative fantasies are often quite far removed from so-called reality; they are as unreal, and as true, as fairy tales and myths. Analysts use imaginative images to grasp the nature of the other person—much as a legend like that of William Tell may grasp and describe the nature of old Switzerland just as well as may careful historical research. Even if they are not expressed, fantasies also influence the other person, awakening new potential in him.

Such creative fantasies have little to do with projections which are autistic. In transference, we project onto our partner images, problems or possibilities related to ourselves or our life histories. Transference images have little to do with the other person. But the creative fantasies I have described are related to the nature of the other person. They represent, in symbolic mythological form, his life potential.

Certain fantasies of parents may serve as an illustration. Parents often indulge, consciously or half-consciously, in fantasies about their children's future. These daydreams are not infrequently wishes of the parents translated into fantasies about their children; they may have a great deal to do with the parents but little to do with the children's actual potentialities. However these fantasies often spring from a basically correct view of a child and represent a creative sighting of his latent potential. A child may not grow up to be the Chief of State, as his mother imagined, but may indeed have great political abilities. He may not become another Picasso but should, in fact, choose a profession which calls for artistic capabilities.

Another example is a young bride often views her husband's future in a highly imaginative manner. Although he is only a social worker, she may daydream that he is a professor or the rector of a university. In these fantasies she may be recognizing a certain academic potential hidden in her husband who might someday actually become a lecturer at a school for social work. The bride's fantasies, in this case, are much related to her husband and to the realization of his potential; her hopes may be unrealistic, but her view is essentially adapted to her partner's nature.

These creative fantasies, this imaginative circumambulating of one's partner, are of the greatest importance in every human relationship. Even when they are strongly mixed with ego-oriented components, they at least serve to stimulate the other person's imagination. Everyone needs to fantasize about himself, to circle about and awaken his own potential in mythological or fairy tale form. One of the tragedies in the lives of orphanage children is that no one weaves such fantasies around them, so that frequently none are awakened in them about their own life potentials; such children may grow up to be well-behaved adults, but they are only half alive psychically.

It should be emphasized again that fantasies of this kind are never "true" in the realistic sense, but definitely so in the symbolic. They may be related to the entire person or just to certain characteristics; they may revolve around past or future possibilities. In everyday conversation they crop up in such statements as, "I could imagine him as an old-time pirate," or "He seems the artistic type to me," or "I can just see him as an English Lord."

The negative effect of fantasies which, while about another person are in reality ego-centered, is well known in the field of education. Many children are nearly destroyed by believing that they must live up to parental fantasies which are not appropriate to them. But seldom is anything said about the positive effect of fantasies which are related to another. Just as, a few decades ago, fairy tales and myths were regarded as nonsense or even as harmful, there was equally a lack of understanding about the importance of fantasizing in education and in interpersonal relations.

To grasp the significance of such mutual fantasies in analysis in particular, and in human relations in general, let us first look briefly at how Jungian psychology regards the action and reaction between two people. It is immediately evident that a person's fantasies about himself exert an influence on him. But it is somewhat more difficult to see how fantasies about another person can influence that person without their being verbalized. Jungian psychology comprehends a relation between two people as more than a contact between two consciousnesses. When two people meet, the totality of their psyches encounter each other; conscious and unconscious, spoken and unspoken; all have their effect upon the other. We do not know precisely how this happens. But it can be observed time and again that one person's psyche has its effect upon the other, with all its desires, fantasies, feelings, and emotions, its consciousness and unconsciousness—even if much of what happens in the psyche is neither stated nor directly expressed.

This concept of relationship is naturally difficult to prove. But most interested observers of interpersonal relations, whether psychotherapists or not, are repeatedly struck by how much more transpires and is exchanged between two people than is ever expressed in word or deed.

An analysand is supposed to try to tell his analyst as honestly as possible everything he feels, dreams, and fantasies. This gives the analyst considerable access to the patient's shadow problems. But although the analyst does not tell his dreams and fantasies—these, too, influence both the analysand and the course of the analysis. If the analyst is really interested in keeping on the track of the shadow, he must therefore actively confront and deal with his own fantasies about his patients. It is of no use to play the completely "objective" therapist, to himself or to his patients. This is self-deception Seen from another angle, we might say that if the analyst were a creature functioning with computer like objectivity, his therapeutic effect would almost certainly be nothing, since the therapist exercises his healing function not as a computer but as a human being. Many therapists try to suppress or repress their fantasies about their patients, as if such fantasies were not permissible. But the content of those fantasies, whatever it may be, continues to have its effect. The point is not to avoid one's fantasies. One of the therapist's first tasks is to examine his own fantasies and try to understand them. Analyst and analysand each have their fantasies about the other, each constantly circle the other in their imaginings.

We are concerned here with tracking down the analyst's shadow. A great deal has been written about the dangers of countertransference. The patient is supposed to have a transference to the analyst if possible. It is then the analyst's job to dissolve this transference and follow it back to its sources. This is how one gets at the neurotic complexes. But if the analyst has a countertransference—if he projects figures, characteristics, etc., onto the patient which have little to do with him or are a kind of reply to the initial transference—then further development is blocked. All this is well known, and every conscientious analyst has been trained to recognize transferences and to prevent the occurrence of countertransferences or to dissolve them as quickly as possible.

But the fantasies described earlier are more difficult, and important in regard to shadow phenomena. Here analysts often merely bury their heads in the sand. Little is said about the fantasies we have about our patients, or they are immediately understood as the expression of a counter-transference—and thus misunderstood entirely.

If an analyst has developed a certain relation to his patient—without which no analysis can proceed—he will have fantasies about him, which express his view of the patient and circle around the patient's potential. These fantasies have an influence, just as those of parents influence the child and those of the wife affect the husband.

At this point, a destructive trait often shows itself in the analyst. Strange, negative fantasies may crop up which persist and even give a certain kind of satisfaction. They may revolve around a possible suicide by the patient, or the outbreak of a psychosis, or they may be destructive images of the patient's family or professional life or his health. Such images exert a strange fascination on the analyst. Instead of a positive concern for the patient, they show an enthrallment with his negative potentialities. This is frequently expressed, in conversations between analysts, by the obvious relish with which one tells the other about the grave danger facing a particular patient. These negative fantasies by the analyst are not projections; they refer to actual lines of possible development. The analyst's psychic energy is concentrated on the patient's destructive side and thus stimulates it. It is a kind of "active imagination," as the term is used in Jungian psychology, but one which revolves around the patient's destructive potential—and it can work like a curse on the patient.

A somewhat more magical form of this phenomenon is often described in popular psychology. It is commonly believed that a parent or teacher who believes that a certain child "will come to no good—he'll probably end up in jail," can exercise a devastating influence on the child. This "negative faith" is a close analogy to the destructive fantasies we have been discussing.

The psychological origins of this almost compulsive revolving around a patient's negative potential are manifold. Among them is the destructive charlatan shadow of the analyst, which is basically not interested in the patient's well-being. But such fantasies are often so destructive that they in fact harm the analyst himself, since an obvious failure in therapy will affect him as well. The nearly compulsive concentration on the patient's negative possibilities is linked to a destructive side in the analyst which we will have to examine later in greater detail.

The therapist is not alone with his negative fantasies, for they are encouraged and influenced by his patients. An analysand's view of his analyst is often correct in a certain respect, but one-sided. He sees possibilities in the analyst which are truly present but which do not constitute the entire picture. His fantasies often revolve around the analyst's shadow. The patient may see him as a money hungry cynic who ridicules his poor clients when talking to his colleagues or as a cold blooded scientist to whom people are of interest only as "cases" or as a bad husband and poor father. And with these negative fantasies, the patient robs the analyst, to a certain extent, of the ability to help him. I want to emphasize once more that we are not speaking here of transference or projections, but of the recognition of real potential in the analyst, a sighting of his shadow.

RELATIONSHIP IS FANTASY

Positive fantasies by the analyst can also be of a destructive character, but their dangerousness is difficult to recognize. As soon as he enters a relationship with a patient, the analyst must somehow fantasy about his future possibilities. It is almost impossible for him just to be there with the patient, see him as he is at the moment, perhaps grasp the psychodynamics of his life story, without also somehow extending his view to the future. Half-conscious fantasies and daydreams must now and then project the patient into the future as "cured" or at least changed. If this does not happen, the patient is not stimulated along these lines and then is in roughly the same situation as the institutionalized orphan child of whom we spoke earlier, around whom no hopeful fantasies of the future are woven and who therefore fails to develop fully for lack of stimulation.

The situation becomes grave when the analyst's imaginings persist in revolving around a patient's possibilities, the development of which would benefit the analyst more than the patient. An example is called for here: an analyst "sees" his patient as a future General Manager. In this particular case, the fantasy is actually in accord with one of the patient's possible lines of development—but it is a possibility which can only be realized if the patient's psychic development proceeds one-sidedly. Thus, it will not necessarily be to the patient's overall benefit if he concentrates on attaining this position of power. But it would help the analyst somehow, giving him an influential connection, a sense of his own power, to see a former patient in a powerful position.

CHAPTER FIVE
The Analyst and the Patient's Extra-Analytical Life

Fed from a number of sources, the destructive side of the analyst appears in remarkably clear and delineated form with regard to his patients' extra-analytical human relations. In some sense every relationship is partially inimical to another. There is a certain claim to exclusivity in most human relations. This also applies to the analytical relationship between therapist and patient. The claim to exclusivity is intensified by the analyst's charlatan shadow, which would like to have the patient completely under its control. In this sense, the analyst's view of the patient's relations to husband or wife, to friends and acquaintances, is often blatantly negative. Only the destructive sides of the patient's human relations are seen, taken up in fantasy, and worked out. Here again, we are not dealing with countertransference. The analyst in such a case is not projecting anything onto the analysand; he is merely directing the spotlight of his mind onto the unhappier aspects of the patient's various interpersonal relations and circling about them with his imagination. People in the patient's environment often notice this, complaining that psychotherapy has only isolated him, and that he now neglects his personal relations and no longer takes them so seriously. Such complaints are not always completely justified, but they often contain a germ of truth. An analyst must work hard in order to prevent the analytical relationship from repeatedly becoming hostile toward other relations. Many a sound friendship has been broken by an analysis; many relationships between husband and wife, parents and children, etc., have been negatively altered by analysis to the detriment of the patient. Somewhere in the analyst's soul there is a bogeyman who wants sole domination of his patients.

Similarly, some analysts try with every means to keep their patients away from group therapy. It often happens that analysts order their analysands—whether they are patients or student analysts—to abandon therapy groups declaring that such groups distract the patient from his personal analysis. For the sake of consistency, they should also order their analysands to leave their wives and children since these are also a source of distraction.

Another mode of the therapist's charlatan shadow is "vicarious living." Under the pretext of healing, the patient is often drained, sucked dry. Patients tell the analyst many things, permitting him to participate in the drama, the tragedies, and joys of their lives. Much of what is experienced by the patient cannot be directly experienced by the analyst. A young man tells of his love affairs, a middle aged woman of the difficulties and delights she has with her children. Taken together, the experiences of all the patients of any given analyst add up to a rich and fascinating spectrum of human life. The analyst may be completely absorbed in his work with his patients, which at first glance would seem a good thing. His own private life takes a back seat to the problems and difficulties of his patients. But a point may be reached where the patients might actually live for the analyst, so to speak, where they are expected to fill the gap left by the analyst's own loss of contact with warm, dynamic life. The analyst no longer has his own friends; his patients' friendships and enmities are as his own. The analyst's sex life may be stunted; his patients' sexual problems provide a substitute. Having chosen such a profession, he is barred from attaining a powerful political position; his investment of energy is all the greater in the power struggles of a politician-patient. In this way, the analyst gradually ceases to lead a vital life and contents himself with the lives of his patients.

First of all this kind of situation is dangerous for the analyst himself. His own psychic development comes to a standstill. Even in his nonprofessional life, he can talk of nothing but his patients and their problems. He is no longer able to love and hate, to invest himself in life, to struggle, to win and lose. His own affective life becomes a surrogate. Acting thus as a quack who draws his sustenance from the lives of his patients, the analyst may seem momentarily to flourish psychically. But in reality he loses his own vitality and creative originality. The advantage of such vicarious living, of course, is that the analyst is also spared any genuine suffering. In a sense this function, too, is exercised for him by others.

Such an analyst is also harmful to his own patients. They too cease to lead genuine lives and instead live only in relation to the analyst experiencing things primarily in order to tell them to him. Love, for instance, becomes not an experience in itself, but something the "how and why" of which can be told to the analyst. The existential beauty of life enriches not the patient but the analyst. Every life may be regarded as a work of art. But in this case the patient no longer creates his life in order to enjoy it himself, but in order that the analyst need not create his work of art, need not invest himself, and instead can take his pleasure in the works of the patient.

It is exceedingly difficult to pin down this phenomenon of vicarious living. In many cases, an analyst who still enjoys and suffers in his own dynamic life has a guilty conscience, feeling that he should really be more interested in his patients. But actually, in the long run, only an analyst who is passionately engaged in his own life can help his patients to find theirs. In this sense it is true, as Jung says, that an analyst can only give to his patients that which he has himself.

CHAPTER SIX
Sexuality And Analysis

The way in which the analyst's shadow appears in the sexual realm is to some extent well known. But it would be worthwhile to examine certain aspects more closely here. I have no intention of launching into a dissertation on the nature of sexuality. But before we turn to the relation between the shadow and sexuality, I should like to make a few general remarks relevant to our subject.

Biologically, sexuality is linked to reproduction. But reproduction and sexuality must be understood as two distinct phenomena. A separation between the two may be observed even in the most primitive living creatures in which reproduction consists of division while sexuality is represented by the flowing together of two organisms. However we are concerned here not with biology but with psychology. The fact is that by far the greater part of human sexual activity takes place without the remotest intention of creating offspring. Nor can we resort to the statement that a woman—if not a man—unconsciously wishes to conceive a child each time she has intercourse. This is a dogmatic assertion which can never be verified by available psychological material. For a long time Christianity, and particularly the Catholic Church, made it a moral law that sexuality must be coupled with reproduction. But modern theology is beginning to see sexuality as something quite different, and psychologically we cannot understand sexuality just in terms of reproduction. It is rather, the expression of a relationship between two people.

Virtually all of human life is played out on a scale ranging between the two poles of body and soul. Every relationship between two people has a bodily aspect: man-woman, mother-child, father-child, woman-to-woman, or man-to-man A mother loves to have physical contact with her child, to stroke and embrace it. A child needs such physical stimulation without which it can never develop a sound sense of the importance of its body. The mother's joy in the child's body is also her joy in the child.

But let us immediately move on to the man-woman relationship. Here sexuality is not the basis for the relationship, but only the physical expression of a fundamental relation between the masculine and feminine which is deeply rooted in humanity. Sexuality is thus the physical aspect of the *mysterium conjunctionis*. A man and a woman do not attract one another in order to create a child. The child is, so to speak, a by-product of this attraction, which is used by nature for reproductive purposes, among other things. Basically, however, the bodily relation between man and woman, the sexual link, is nothing other than one of the most intense links between the masculine and feminine.

I have already mentioned several times that in the psychotherapeutic situation, a relationship must arise. Without this the patient cannot develop. If absolutely no emotion, no affect, flows between patient and therapist, the psychic process cannot get moving. Every psychotherapy is predicated on, at least, a minimal relationship. If it is present, it is not only psychic but must have a bodily or physical component as well. The physical relation between analyst and patient is important.

But every human relation may be negative or positive—
a fact which those who would like to make a religion of
interpersonal relations do not want to recognize. There is
love and hate in every relationship, a desire to help the
other and at the same time to destroy him. One or the
other of these factors may predominate, love or hate, Eros
or destructiveness. Unfortunately, in common parlance,
sexuality—that is the physical relation between man and
woman—is often referred to as "love." This is just as senseless as it would be to use the word love to describe any
and every relation between people. Sexuality, the bodily
aspect of human relations, can express love and hate. I am
speaking here of "normal" sexual relations and not of such
deviations as sadomasochism in which the situation is more
or less clear. Normal sexuality springing from hate, yet
understood as love, has destroyed countless people, and it
can do the greatest damage to analyst and patient in
psychotherapy. Sexual desire often crops up in patients
and analysts. (For the sake of simplicity, in the following
paragraphs I will assume a male analyst and female
patient, although the same ideas apply in the reverse situation.) It is a commonplace that women patients often
have sexual desires and fantasies revolving around the
analyst. But there is less willingness to discuss the fact that
analysts likewise often spin sexual fantasies around their
patients. This phenomenon is, unfortunately, always viewed
in the light of transference and countertransference. But it
seems to me far more important to comprehend the sexual
desires and fantasies of patients and analysts as physical
expressions of relationship. However in doing so we must
remain aware that relationship always has a double aspect. Relationship means Eros and hate, with one or
another dominating, depending on circumstances.

As far as sexual fantasies are concerned, Jungian analysts may perhaps be a bit bolder than therapists of other schools. They do not immediately attack such fantasies as transference or countertransference phenomena and are quite capable not only of pacifying their patients but also of challenging them to go right on having sexual fantasies and to see how they develop. But to do this it must first be determined whether this activation of sexuality in the therapeutic situation is an expression of a negative or a positive relationship. Quite often, for example, a patient's sexual longing for her analyst is nothing more than her desire to destroy him professionally, a desire which in turn is a result of her particular psychic state. We cannot here deal with the many reasons why a patient might wish to destroy her analyst. But the fact remains that this destructively impelled activation of sexuality often constellates an equally destructive sexuality in the analyst. It is one of the oldest charlatan tricks to try to bind women patients by awakening sexual desire. It is easy for a psychotherapist to fall into this particular shadow aspect, and it is frequently reinforced by something even more uncanny: self-destructiveness. This self-destructive tendency has already been mentioned earlier in this book, and we will return to it later. If the constellated sexuality is an expression of destructive forces, it is vital for the analyst to pursue it, in himself and in the patient, with great psychological earnestness. More than a few analysts have destroyed themselves and their patients by living out this sexuality—a kind of sexuality which pushes almost compulsively to be lived out, precisely in order to destroy.

The situation is different when the awakening of sexual desire in patient and analyst is an expression, a bodily aspect, of a basically positive relationship. This is far less dangerous, since neither party is essentially interested in destroying the other, and the sexual fantasies are nothing other than the expression of a fruitful relationship which is bound to have a positive effect on the therapy. Such fantasies may be safely permitted to continue and to develop, for the urge to live them out is not so strong.

About the living out of sexual fantasies: it is an iron rule of analysis that sexuality between analyst and patient must under no circumstances be lived out, regardless of the marital status of those concerned. But, of course, the fundamental correctness of even such iron-clad rules must be repeatedly questioned and examined. There are patients, and even some analysts, who argue that, since relationship plays such a decisive role in therapy, it might theoretically happen sometimes that a relationship can only attain its full therapeutic value when it is also lived out sexually. I believe this to be based on a misunderstanding. The object of therapy is not the relationship between analyst and analysand, but the healing of the patient through the establishment of a new psychic orientation. If the relationship is lived out sexually, it becomes no longer only the vessel in which the healing process takes place, it becomes an end in itself and thus destroys the therapy. Consciously or semi-consciously, this is perfectly clear to the analyst and generally also to the patient. Therefore it may be taken as a rule that the more a patient or something in the analyst pushes for living out the sexual side of the relationship, the more probable it is that the sexuality is destructive. It is destructive with regard to the therapy, and quite certainly also expressive of a relationship which is destructive in general. An attempt is being made to destroy the therapist as therapist. Yet the therapist is an important part of the man whom the patient claims to love. Hence a living out of sexuality and the therapeutic situation under no circumstances go hand in hand.

But although there must be an irrevocable "No" to the living out of sexuality in analysis, the attitude toward the appearance of a mutual sexual attraction should be more differentiated. The question must be repeatedly investigated of what this sexuality really expresses. The analyst must constantly and painstakingly examine his own as well as his patient's sexual fantasies; merely to understand those of the patient and to suppress his own, is of questionable value. For the actual character of the psychic situation is partly mirrored in his own fantasies.

For example a psychologist who was controlling a case with a colleague reported this recurring fantasy. He has sexual intercourse with a patient. On the following day she has to be committed to a private psychiatric clinic due to an attack of hysterical screaming. At the clinic she shouts out an account of what happened between her and her analyst. This fantasy raises at least the suspicion that certain destructive factors were at work behind the sexual feelings of both analyst and patient.

Jungian psychotherapists in particular demonstrate a unique form of the charlatan shadow. It was one of Jung's many achievements that, rather than discounting or disproving Freud's discoveries in the realm of sexuality, he gave them deeper meaning. A Jungian psychologist comprehends sexuality fundamentally as a symbol of something non-sexual; a symbol of the unification of opposites, the *conjunctio oppositorum.* The love letters of a nun to Jesus are not necessarily the sublimation of a wild sexual drive but precisely the reverse. Even the most primitive form of sexuality is to a certain extent a lived symbol of the unification of those polar oppositions which are an eternal source of pain and joy to humanity.

Thus, in the final analysis, the phenomenon of intense erotic and sexual attraction in psychotherapy should also be understood as a symbol of the unification of opposites; as a lived *mysterium conjuntionis.* This transcendent aspect of the intense attraction between analyst and patient must be somehow grasped and experienced by both parties during analysis.

But precisely this transcendental aspect of the phenomenon can be used by the analyst's charlatan shadow as a dodge. Every analyst is more or less aware that the constellation of sexuality harbors many dangers. Destructive sexuality works like an infectious disease. An anxious Jungian analyst, concerned only for his own welfare, often side-steps the dangers of sexuality by immediately pointing to the transcendental aspect as soon as any sexual feelings crop up. He gives careful attention neither to his own fantasies nor to those of his patient but instead takes instant refuge in the deeper symbolism of the sexual phenomenon. This gives him a certain immunity against the dangers raised by an aroused sexuality. But it also destroys certain possibilities of relationship and spoils an opportunity of dealing with possible destructive tendencies in himself and his patient. Despite his good intentions he also devalues the patient's experience and perhaps his own as well.

Though sexuality is ultimately a symbol, it can only be a living symbol if it is truly experienced. Psychological and philosophical formulations come between the person and the experience. Moreover, the premature emphasis on the symbol awakens in the patient a sense of not being taken seriously. She is, at the moment, plagued and lured by sexual fantasies and desires. The analyst must first be able to understand them, and in a certain sense, to share the experience before he tries to enrich it with its profound symbolism.

CHAPTER SEVEN
The Destructive Fear Of Homosexuality

Homosexual attraction presents a far more complicated relatedness problem in analysis than does heterosexual attraction. But before going into this in greater detail, a few brief remarks on homosexuality in general are necessary.

Many psychologists assume that the child is "polymorphously perverse," which includes, among other sexual "deviations," both heterosexuality and homosexuality. Sexual play among children obviously takes place on both levels. In the course of development, the heterosexual component steadily gains in importance while the homosexual recedes into the background, is suppressed, and repressed. In many people the homosexual side is close to the surface and may temporarily be activated under certain circumstances. Many psychologists believe that homosexuality is often so close to the surface that it must be sublimated in some form. They feel that people such as youth leaders, teachers, military officers, etc., frequently demonstrate homosexuality which has been sublimated into an interest in young men, students, and so on. In *The Platonic Dialogues*, Socrates takes a somewhat different position. He maintains that homosexuality is actually a higher form of love, not coupled with the reproductive drive and therefore purer and more worthy of man.

Earlier I pointed out that every relationship has a physical or bodily aspect. Two people in a relationship, regardless of whether they are of the same or different sex, must feel something physical for one another. In most relationships the body is involved somehow. This bodily feeling between two people of the same sex is often characterized as latent homosexuality and "pathologized" as something which should not be.

But perhaps homosexuality should be defined somewhat differently. A homosexual is one who rejects the longing and need for union with the human polarity (feminine-masculine), who is not capable of it because the other, the contra-sexual, frightens him and he feels himself inadequate to it for some psychodynamic reasons. Consequently, he channels everything that should go to the opposite sex into the—basically normal—bodily feelings toward those of the same sex. Thus, in most cases, the homosexual has repressed his heterosexuality. Part of his heterosexual psychic energy now flows into a homosexuality which, in essence, has always been present.

In speaking of sublimated or latent homosexuality, we are often misunderstanding the situation. Frequently it is not a case of homosexuality in the sense in which I have just described it, but simply the presence of a strong, unconditioned Eros. Let us be more concrete.

Two men who like each other, or two women who are friends, must not find one another physically repulsive. No one can have someone for a friend whose physical presence repels him. He must take pleasure in eating with his friend, walking with him, hearing him breathe. Not only must he not feel repelled by the other's body, he must himself feel some sense of physical well-being in the other's bodily presence. A friend must find the other's bodily aspect somehow pleasant. Perhaps, in the long run, it is this erotic feeling of which Socrates spoke. He repeatedly implied that he had hardly ever engaged in homosexual acts but had merely experienced erotic feelings.

For certain historical reasons, which the scope of this paper does not permit us to delineate, this bodily aspect of relationships between people of the same sex is strictly taboo in most cultures today, suppressed from childhood and regarded as thoroughly reprehensible. Northern peoples in particular are extreme in their rejection of the bodily aspect of relationship. Among southern peoples it is still common, and perfectly acceptable, for men to embrace and to have bodily contact. During the Romantic epoch it was possible to see male friends strolling hand in hand. Now, among us Swiss, for example, bodily contact among so-called normal men is possible only under the influence of alcohol.

Analysis makes use of relationship for therapy. But since an intensive relationship also constellates physical feelings between two men or two women, analyst and analysand must be, in some sense, bodily "together," must experience the same vibrations. Few analysts can stand up to this. As soon as bodily vibrations are felt, whether in fantasies or dreams, there is talk of latent homosexuality and the matter becomes painful to the analyst. The bodily side of Eros is shoved aside and destroyed.

Jungian psychologists may, however, try to evade this involvement in Eros by not following up veiled or even relatively overt sexual statements by the patient or by immediately trying to interpret such statements on a "higher level." They make reference to the patient's relation to the spiritual masculine, to his own creative masculinity, etc. A homosexual dream is instantly interpreted as "a search for, and an attempt to understand, one's own masculinity."

61

As in the case of heterosexual eroticism, the analyst here, too, is trying to evade erotic phenomena. He feels them to be dangerous, clothes himself in an endless variety of theories, and runs for cover. An example: an analysand dreams that he is caressing and embracing the analyst. The analyst probably finds this dream painful and repugnant and interprets it on the objective level as an expression of latent homosexuality. On the subjective level he expresses it as the patient's caressing of his own inner therapeutic factor (analyst equals therapeutic factor). Perhaps, however, the dream simply expresses the analysand's desire to draw closer to the analyst, physically and psychically. The analyst is being called upon to give his patient tenderness. His use of interpretations as a screen behind which to reject such a request is of no use whatsoever to the patient.

This rejection of the bodily aspect by the analysand, and even more particularly by the analyst, has serious consequences. Part of the erotic feeling is stumbling around in the dark, so to speak. The relationship between analyst and patient may be transformed into one of hatred and rejection. The analysis may have to be broken off, or it may be brought to a laborious conclusion. The relation is now characterized on both sides by paranoid suspicions. In the Freudian sense, both parties have repressed their so-called homosexuality, and both feel threatened by it, so that each feels persecuted by the other.

When such bodily feelings are constellated, the serious analyst, who is willing to expose himself to danger, has no choice, He must not reject such feelings but must follow them up and permit his patient to fantasize. At the very least he must accept his patient's fantasies, rather than labelling them as pathological or fending them off by pointing to their ultimate symbolic significance.

Psychotherapy is, in the last analysis, an erotic activity. But the analyst's charlatan shadow tries to avoid erotic demands. At most it is erotically related to itself but not to the patient.

CHAPTER EIGHT
The Analyst as Flatterer

The charlatan shadow which urges the analyst to avoid the interpersonal demands of analysis often expresses itself in another, highly unexpected manner. An analyst must frequently say hard things to his patient. They are obligated to point out psychological mechanisms and hidden pitfalls, which may be painful to the analyst, but even more so to the patient. Both of them bear this burden, however, if the statements are made in a spirit of truth and genuineness. At this point two dangers arise.

The first is that the analyst can use the necessity of making hurtful observations in order to torture his patient and demonstrate his own power. If he does so, however, the analyst usually feels it rather quickly. He experiences a sense of guilt and, after honest self-evaluation, realizes what has happened.

The second possibility is more dangerous. The analyst may begin to transform his unpleasant observations about the patient into flattery. This looks like a genuine reaching out to the patient and may satisfy both parties momentarily. In fact, the patient may even be helped for the moment in his psychological development by an increase in self-esteem. In the process, however, the analyst binds the patient more firmly to himself, since in the latter's eyes he has become someone who apparently sees the greatest value in something which might not appear so valuable at first glance.

Here are a few examples the "archetype of the queen" is explained to a decidedly power hungry woman; the over-dominating aspect of the feminine is interpreted as an expression of a "royal nature." The lack of courage in interpersonal relations, fear of love or even the inability to love, may be interpreted as "interesting introversion;" the patient is not labeled a ruthless egoist but a noble introvert. An egoistic lack of respect for an aging mother is understood as liberation from the mother's animus. Instead of trying to ease the tense relationship between father and child, there is talk of "the king must die," of the necessary murder of the primal father. No mention is made of the fact that a careful analysis can often transform threatening parents into friendly old people whose menace disappears as the patient grows stronger in himself. An effeminate nineteen year old who has succeeded in extorting a sports car from his wealthy father is praised for his firmness toward the old man and the sports car is regarded as a symbol of newly acquired masculinity.

It is difficult for an analyst to avoid uttering such flattery now and again. It is, after all, his legitimate aim to show the patient that he is indeed a worthwhile human being, and to point up the fascinating aspects of the psyche at work behind all neurotic difficulties. The patient must be given the justified feeling that his life and his soul are as valuable and interesting as those of anyone else. On the purely verbal level, there is often only a slight difference between highlighting the patient's genuine psychic values on the basis of flattery and doing so in all truth and sincerity. Mere nuances are of paramount importance. If flattery dominates, the patient will become a neurotic who glorifies his distorted side, which is disruptive and destructive for his environment and in the long run for himself as well.

His psychological development, which is based on veracity, will be severely disturbed. When an analyst begins to flatter, he will rarely get any help from his patient. On the contrary, in such situations the patient generally also begins to flatter the analyst directly or indirectly. This mutual flattery is not a matter of transference and countertransference, but simply that analyst and analysand lull one another, seem able to work beautifully together, mutually enhance each other's self-esteem—and in reality permit the serious business of analysis to degenerate into a charlatan's game. The deeper value of psychic development is betrayed.

CHAPTER NINE
The Abuse of the Search for Meaning

In Jungian analysis the concept of the self plays a central role. In a certain sense the self is a counter-pole to the ego. The ego is concerned with worldly man, with social and familial position, with physical health and emotional soundness. The self, on the other hand, is often described as the "divine spark" in humanity. In rather solemn terms one might say that it is concerned with the eternal values of the human psyche. The self is not primarily concerned with social position, success in business, personal relations, and a long life span, etc., but rather with that which Christianity has termed "Christ within us." In Christian parlance the ego is often characterized as "world" while the self is indicated by the concept of "soul."

The differentiation between self and ego is of extraordinary importance and no analysis can be successfully concluded without this difference having been experienced in some form or other. But here an opening is presented to the charlatan shadow: current morality, concepts of honor, loyalty, respectability, marital fidelity, are in many respects products of the ego of Western humanity and not of the self. Seen from a loftier vantage point, there are times when the nonmoral is that which must be done. Such infractions of generally accepted morality range from harmless "white lies" to the murder of another person. The individual is repeatedly confronted with decisions which cannot be made within the framework of general moral rules but which require taking a personal stand, in some cases involving a breach of the rules. This can lead to severe conflicts.

Every analyst knows this. The self may make its own claims on the ego. But often this fact is used to justify, with the analyst's help, simply immoral, unkind, or aggressive behavior on the part of the patient. Adultery, for example, may be interpreted not primarily as a serious insult to and attack upon the spouse but as a liberation from collective norms in the name of the self and under the banner of self-realization. Unfair and disloyal behavior towards friends, acquaintances, employees or superiors, the rejection of morality and virtue, are lauded as a bold redemption from the collective, as emotional independence. In this way the analyst helps his patient to achieve momentary relief from certain moral conflicts. The adulterer or the disloyal friend no longer feels guilty. The patient is happy to have rid himself of his moral conflict in this deceptively simple manner. But in the long run it will do him no good since his relief has been obtained at the cost of truthfulness. For his part, the analyst is happy to have found a simple, quick way to a "cure." The charlatan in him urges him to avoid the long, difficult path to a genuine cure. In this case his concern is not for the true healing of the patient but for his own image as a great healer.

Earlier in this book I described how both analyst and patient often fall temporarily into the pattern of sorcerer and sorcerer's apprentice. At the outset this constellation may even be necessary to some extent, and in some cases it may be dissolved again without difficulty. But in the course of an analysis, the sorcerer appears in a somewhat different and far more dangerous form. He may amalgamate with what I characterized in the previous chapter as the false prophet. The analyst trapped in the false-prophet-cum-sorcerer shadow begins to allay the patient's religious needs with the pretense of transcendental knowledge. He sees demonstrable meaning in all events. Such a Jungian analyst, for example, might demonstrate in everything the workings of the unconscious. Every dream, every event or happenstance, every ailment and suffering, every joy, every accident, and every stroke of luck is understood meaningfully in terms of the unconscious. Like a little god the analyst sees everything clearly and can trace every event back to something or other. The dark hand of the Moirae, the Fates, to which even the gods (i.e., the unconscious) are subject, is no longer acknowledged; there is no longer any tragedy, any incomprehensible horror. People fall into misfortune solely because they have lost contact with the unconscious or because they do not know themselves. And in the end such analysts even pretend to their patients that they can see behind the scenes of world events.

It matters not in the least to which theoretical school an analyst belongs. Any analyst, on the basis of his particular theory, can pretend to himself and his patient that he is capable of penetrating every event. In a magical, artistic, and prophetic manner he can try to link anything and everything to those basic forces which he believes govern psychic life. This procedure gives the patient a momentary sense of security and the analyst a pleasant sense of himself as an omniscient magician.

The analyst's charlatan shadow appears in many other guises as well. Volumes could be filled describing them. I have tried to point up just a few concrete examples. But it is also important to see how this charlatan shadow always crops up simultaneously or in conjunction with certain of the patient's destructive tendencies regarding therapy. The two phenomena stimulate or reinforce one another. For this reason, the analyst cannot track down the patient's resistant shadow and its destructiveness for therapy without persistently being aware of his own shadow. This links up to the reference made in the chapter, "Psychotherapist, Charlatan and False Prophet," concerning the need for honesty on the part of the analyst toward the patient. We must refrain from playing the part of someone who never falls into the shadow and must be prepared to admit our mistakes in this regard, not necessarily in every case, but certainly in principle. The patient's destructive resistances are linked to our own shadow problems, and one cannot really be grasped without the other. For example, we must be willing to say: "Here we both fell into our destructive tendencies. I tried to flatter you, and you tried to aggrandize your own neurotic complexes and make yourself appear interesting as a neurotic."

Shadow in the analyst constellates shadow in the patient. Our own honesty helps the patient to confront his shadow phenomena. Each of us must work on both areas.

I have now dealt at some length with the problems of the psychotherapist. In the earlier chapter, "Social Work and Inquisition," I described some difficulties encountered by the social worker. To expand our understanding of the dark sides of these two activities, perhaps it is necessary to go into what it is that drives the members of these professions to do the kind of work they do. What prompts the psychotherapist to try to help people in emotional difficulty? What motivates the psychiatrist to deal with the mentally ill? Why does the social worker concern himself with social misfits? What is it that compels people to want to help the sick, the suffering, the unhappy, the outcast?

In order to understand these matters, we must first examine the situation of the doctor—the primal image of the helper and healer. Perhaps a view of the doctor's shadow aspect and his basic model of the helper-healer, whether he be psychiatrist, psychotherapist, analyst, or social worker, is ultimately derived from classical medicine. To the extent that a welfare worker functions purely as a dispenser of alms, his activity has little to do with the medical image. But modern social work has moved, we might say, in a medical direction. A social worker today is not there to give charity but to help heal a social situation. And the modern social worker tries—sometimes almost too zealously—to derive from psychology knowledge which can help him aid the social outcast. Case work today often comes close to simplified psychotherapy.

CHAPTER TEN
The Powerful Doctor and the Childish Patient

At the start of this book, we were concerned with the problem of power in social welfare work. The dark phenomenon of the power drive in social work is obvious to everyone active in this field. But the power problem is just as obtrusive in the medical profession.

Medicine has made great progress during the past century. There has been a tremendous increase in its ability to ameliorate suffering and prevent illness. Many infectious diseases, such as the plague, have been practically obliterated. The use of vaccine has virtually eliminated epidemic or endemic smallpox. Tuberculosis has been brought partially under control. Technical progress in surgery has made possible the most extraordinary life saving and life prolonging operations: arms can be sewed on, hearts replaced. The old scourge of childbed fever, which victimized so many young women, is a rarity today. In imagination, at least, we see the limits of medicine only on the remote horizon. Its tools and facilities are such that it is obvious to suspect the modern doctor of having a great deal of power, in both the positive and negative sense.

The archaic doctor was the medicine man with whose traits we are familiar from the descriptions of ethnologists. These make it clear that medicine men were always regarded as powerful figures who did not hesitate to resort to any means in order to retain this power. The medicine man's power, and lust for power, was linked to the fact that he was not only a doctor but a priest in contact with higher forces. Anyone interested in history is aware that among those who were assumed to be in direct touch with the gods, there have always been some who have misused their power.

Also, doctors of ancient Greece were priests—but priests of Asclepius, a god of healing, (who in the course of time became merely a patron saint). Arab and Jewish physicians of the Middle Ages had developed along a path widely divergent from that of the priesthood and were doctors very nearly in the modern sense. Medieval European physicians came under the influence of alchemy and thus were once more in contact with the supernatural. The doctors of the Renaissance worked again more as "pure" doctors, rather as scientists than as priests.

Throughout those historical periods in which medical means were limited and in which doctors had already separated themselves from the priesthood, they were nevertheless almost as respected and feared as are physicians today. Indeed, it often seems as if the doctors had as much power as the priests. But is the power of the doctor, of medicine in general, then, not more closely linked to psychological power than to power based on scientific knowledge?

Let us approach this subject from a psychological angle. Healthy people can lead an independent life, dignified, and respectable. A healthy body enables a person to pursue his affairs freely and independently, provided that outside circumstances are favorable. But all this is changed when sickness intervenes. Then the healthy man becomes a patient, and the adult is transformed into a child. The formerly dignified, healthy individual is suddenly dominated by fear, tortured by pain, and threatened by death. A strange form of regression takes place. A patient is no longer the master of his body but its victim. The psyche, too, seems to be transformed under the influence of bodily illness. Women who have had to nurse their temporarily sick husbands can relate countless examples of this change. The strong man, protector of the home and master of the house, becomes a child calling with tearful voice for his orange juice. Doctors and nurses see the same regression in hospitalized patients, see adults grow childish, with blind trust in their specialists alternating with equally childish recalcitrance.

In such a situation the doctor becomes the great helper. He is the source of all hope. Feared, respected, hated, and admired, he seems at times an almost god-like redeemer. The doctor can heal, can ease pain, and make the experience of death bearable. The patient is lost without him.

Purely intellectually, of course, the doctor knows that his patients are people like himself. But the honest physician must frequently admit to himself the impossibility of avoiding a negative attitude toward his patients. Especially to a hospital doctor, patients often become poor, unhappy creatures without status or dignity, virtually a different class of human being. They are often unreasonable, do not take their medicine, do things harmful to themselves, sometimes obey, and sometimes do not—just like little children. A polarity takes shape with the regressed, childish, fearful patient at one end, and at the other, the superior, proud physician, aloof though perhaps still somewhat coolly courteous.

CHAPTER ELEVEN
The "Healer-Patient" Archetype and Power

The "healer-patient" relationship is as fundamental as is that of man-woman, father-son, mother-child. It is archetypal in the sense expounded by Jung; i.e. it is an inherent, potential form of human behavior. In archetypal situations the individual perceives and acts in accordance with a basic schema inherent in himself but which in principle is the same for all men. Does power lie hidden somewhere in the archetype of healer-patient? Before we try to answer this question, we must first briefly sketch the many meanings which the word "power" can have.

In a relationship one subject confronts another. Each relates to the other as a subject. In a relationship in which power is a dominant factor, one subject tries to make an object out of the other, while the latter subjects himself to the former. That is, the object can now be manipulated by the subject for his own purposes. Such a situation enhances the subject's sense of his importance and relieves the object of responsibility. This is one kind of power.

Another variety is "self-deification." Only God, or the gods, have the right to dominate men. A human possessed by a "god complex" tries, like a god, to dominate other humans. This kind of power has a numinous quality and is dangerous for both the ruler and the ruled. The Caesars, Napoleon, and Hitler were examples of such self-deification. This is the kind of power which Jakob Burckhardt described as evil.

The modern cult surrounding the physician is at least partly an expression of this power. In using the term cult, I mean the public veneration and social prestige enjoyed by the doctor as he who "has life and death, sickness and health in his hands." It finds expression in novels about doctors, in biographies such as that of San Michele, in popular films, and television series.

This cult and the power which physicians can exercise in hospitals are linked and mutually reinforcing. The dictatorial head doctor, whose moods terrorize patients and before whose every grumble nurses and interns quake, is a familiar figure. Patients do not dare to ask questions for fear of being badly treated. Nevertheless, many nurses, students, and patients admire such a show of power and respect the great, mighty healer as he strides like a demi-god through the hospital corridors followed by a swarm of assistants.

But something is wrong here. A cheap note seems to be creeping into my prose. The medical novels and memoirs, the television plays about hospital life, are generally sentimental, in poor taste, and devoid of any artistic value. There is something impressive about a politician who exercises his power, a union leader who can paralyze an entire industry with a word, an industrial manager whose decisions affect the lives of thousands, a general on whom the life and death of countless soldiers may depend. But a physician who abuses his position to exercise power seems like a ridiculous little tyrant, overblown and morally deplorable. He keeps his patients waiting for hours while he chats leisurely with the nurses, gives the ill a minimum of information about their condition, and issues directives without explanation. He strides through the wards like some oriental potentate overseeing his helpless slaves. All of this seems petty, with nothing splendid about it.

THE "HEALER-PATIENT" ARCHETYPE AND POWER

At this point we face the question of the nature of the physician's power. Health and sickness, the healer and the ill, doctor and patient, are all archetypal motifs. Does power belong to the archetype of healer-patient as it does to the archetype of king-subject? If this were really the case, the exercise of such power would have nothing cheap or mean about it. An archetype is a primal factor, a fundamental reality, and as such it cannot be petty in nature. Or is the kind of power which I have described above in the relation between patient and doctor exclusively negative and destructive, an attempt to make an object of a subject and to degrade the humanity of the partner in the relationship? It does not seem tenable to maintain that we doctors are so strongly guided by destructive forces. We chose our profession in order to be able to heal; it can hardly be assumed that we are primarily driven by such destructive motives. Or are we perhaps dealing with a form of self-deification, with a god complex which is commonly activated in the physician? This would be a possibility, but here again the pettiness and tastelessness of the phenomenon seems to argue against such an assumption. To try to become like God is a great transgression, but it has nothing petty about it. Nevertheless, the paltriness associated with the power of the doctor cannot be a mere matter of chance. The various kinds of power which I have described seem inapplicable to the problem we are considering.

CHAPTER TWELVE
The Splitting of the Archetype

Many diverse characteristics of the archetype have been dealt with in psychological literature. But one aspect seems to have been relatively ignored. In order to avoid misunderstandings, I will, with different words than before, again go into the nature of the archetype.

An archetype may be defined as an inborn potentiality of behavior. Human beings react archetypally to someone or something when faced with a typical, constantly recurring situation. A mother or father reacts archetypally to a son or daughter, a man reacts archetypally to a woman, etc. In this sense certain archetypes have two poles, so to speak. The basic situation of the archetype contains a polarity.

Of course we do not know precisely how archetypal behavior came about. Perhaps one pole of the archetype was originally in the individual and the other pole outside him in other humans. But in psychology as we know it, both poles are contained within the same individual. Each of us is born with both poles of the archetype within us. If one pole of an archetype is constellated in the outside world, the inner and opposite pole is constellated as well.

Many ailments require the ministrations of an external physician. But no physician can be effective without the inner doctor. A physician can stitch up a wound, but something in the patient's body and psyche must help if an ailment is be overcome. It is not difficult to imagine the healing factor in the patient.

But what about the physician? Here we encounter the archetype of the "wounded healer." Chiron, the centaur who taught Asclepius the healing arts, himself suffered from incurable wounds. In Babylon there was a dog-goddess with two names: as Gula she was death, and as Labartu, healing. In India Kali is the goddess of the pox and at the same time its curer. The mythological image of the wounded healer is widespread. Psychologically this means not only that the patient has a physician within himself but also that there is a patient in the doctor.

We began this chapter with the question of power. Let us see if the concept of the split archetype can cast a sharper light on this problem. It is not easy for the human psyche to bear the tension of polarities. The ego loves clarity and tries to eradicate inner ambivalence. This need for the unequivocal can bring about a certain splitting of polar archetypes. One pole may be repressed and continue operating in the unconscious, possibly causing psychic disturbances. The repressed part of the archetype can be projected onto the outer world. The patient, for instance, can project his inner healer on the doctor treating him, and the physician can project his own wounds onto the patient. This projection of one pole of the archetype onto the outer world may bring momentary satisfaction. But in the long run, it means that the psychic process is blocked. In such a situation a patient, for example, may no longer be concerned with his own cure. The doctor, the nurses, the hospital will heal him. The patient no longer has any responsibility. Consciously and unconsciously he begins to rely completely on the doctor to bring about improvement. He hands his own healing over to the doctor, and so to speak, sits back and takes it easy. Such a patient may follow the doctor's orders or not, he may take his medicine or flush it down the drain. The large out-patient clinics swarm with patients like this; they always suffer from something, and there are no signs in them of a will to health or what we might term a conscience of health. They follow the doctor's suggestions or rebel against them, like school children who believe that only the teacher need be active in the process of learning.

In the doctor the repression of one pole of the archetype leads to the reverse situation. He begins to have the impression that weakness, illness, and wounds have nothing to do with him. He feels himself to be the strong healer. The only wounds are those of the patients, while he himself is secure against them. The poor creatures known as patients live in a world completely different from his own. He develops into a physician without wounds and can no longer constellate the healing factor in his patients. He becomes only a doctor, and his patients are only patients. It is no longer the wounded healer who confronts the ill and constellates their inner healing factor. The situation becomes crystal clear: on the one hand there is the doctor, healthy and strong, and on the other hand the patient, sick and weak.

CHAPTER THIRTEEN
The Closing of the Split Through Power

Many doctors choose their profession out of a deep inner need. Even if a physician tries to repress one pole of the archetype, to project illness completely onto the patient and identify himself exclusively with the healer pole, he cannot get off so lightly. Patients, sickness, and wounds leave him no peace; whether he likes it or not, they belong to him. A split archetype tries persistently to return to its original polarity.

Reunification with the missing aspect of the polarity may take place through power. The doctor may turn his patient into an object of his power drive. Now it becomes clear why the power exercised by the physician makes such a cheap and shabby impression. It is the result of a partial psychological and moral failure by both doctor and patient. The doctor is no longer able to see his wounds and potential for illness. He sees sickness only in the other. He objectifies illness, distances himself from his own weakness, elevates himself, and degrades the patient. He becomes powerful through psychological failure rather than through strength. One pole of the archetype is repressed, then projected, then reunited through power. The patient can do precisely the same thing, in the reverse.

At this point we might ask whether there are other cases in which the split polarity of the archetype is rejoined through power. I do not know whether this happens with all archetypes, but it seems to be a frequent phenomenon.

For example, when the mother-daughter archetype is split, the power problem begins to play a dominant role in the relationship between mother and daughter. In practical terms this means that the mother becomes only-a-mother, forgetting that she has an inner daughter as well, something "daughterly" in herself. Instead, she tries to be the perfect mother without weaknesses. In such a case the daughter becomes a total daughter, helpless and completely reliant on the strong mother. The mother rules her daughter with power. No "motherliness" is constellated in the daughter herself; nothing maternal inside her begins to care for herself, and no daughter is constellated in the mother. The relationship is that between a strong, dominating mother and a weak, dependent daughter. The desire for power and the state of subjugation are here the expression of an attempt to reunify the split archetype.

So the physician tries to reunite the split archetype through power and the patient through acknowledgment of this power, through his subjection, or childish dependence. This manifestation of power has its psychologically positive side as well, for the doctor is at least trying to reunite the two poles of the archetype. The petty, tyrannical doctor is in his way wrestling with the fundamental medical problem. In this respect he is better than the jovial healer who no longer even takes the trouble to at least try to dominate his patients. This cheerful, relaxed doctor has either repressed one pole of the archetype so severely that it can no longer be projected, or else he has never really been concerned with the basic problem of the physician and his choice of profession was merely superficial.

However despite this positive aspect, the consequences of the split archetype of the wounded healer are in many respects damaging for both patient and doctor. The sick man becomes the perennial patient; his inner healing factor is no longer activated. The physician becomes a self-important, narrow-minded man blind to his own psychological development. His ability to constellate the healing factor in his patients is greatly reduced; he believes that his primary function is to make it possible for the patient's own inner healing factor to come into play. In a certain respect he becomes a priest who believes that he is far removed from the Greek physician, who maintained that only the divine healer can help while the human doctor merely can facilitate its appearance.

Here we should clarify a possible point of misunderstanding. When I speak of the wounded healer, I do not mean a doctor who identifies himself with the individual patient. That would be pure sentimentality and would constitute only an external reunification of the poles of the archetype. Such an identification is a sign of ego weakness, an hysterical method of uniting the opposites.

The image of the wounded healer symbolizes an acute and painful awareness of sickness as the counter pole to the physician's health, a lasting and hurtful certainty of the degeneration of his own body and mind. This sort of experience makes of the doctor the patient's brother rather than his master. Everyone has within him the health-sickness archetype. But it has a special fascination for the physician with a true vocation. This is why he chooses the medical profession. The average doctor does not enter upon his career for the sake of an easy way to gain power, and perhaps, at the same time to help humanity. Doctors are often accused of being more interested in diseases than in cures. This is a half-truth. Physicians are interested in the health-sickness archetype and wish to experience it. For a great variety of psychological reasons, those men and women who choose a career in medicine are attracted by the healer-patient archetype. Unfortunately, not all of those who choose such a career are strong enough to continually experience both ends of the polarity.

To concretize what we have said thus far, let us take a look at medical students. In the course of their studies they often go through a phase in which they believe themselves to be suffering from all those diseases about which they must learn. They hear about tuberculosis and discover in themselves all its symptoms; they encounter cancer patients and begin to fear that they, too, are suffering from it. This psychological phenomenon is often understood as a neurosis. Older doctors smile at their fear ridden students, recall that they went through a similar phase themselves, and ascribe no importance to it. But this so-called neurotic phase can be a turning point for the medical student. It is the moment when he begins to understand that all these ailments are in himself. Thus he becomes the "wounded healer." However, very often the burden is too great, and the pole of sickness is repressed. But if he is capable of experiencing sickness as an existential possibility in himself, and of integrating it, then the student becomes a true wounded healer.

Once again I wish to caution against the conclusion that power exercised in the medical profession is completely negative. It is true that the more power is exerted, the less the genuine healer appears. But I cannot emphasize often enough that it is better for a doctor to try to reunite the split archetype through power than simply to ignore the split-off pole entirely.

Now let us briefly concern ourselves with today's physician. Modern medicine is highly technical and specialized. Our fantasy of the old country doctor, intimately familiar with his patient's entire family, may serve as the prototype carrier of an unsplit healer-patient archetype. He had no power, but when he arrived feverish children were calmed. Perhaps he wore shabby, rumpled clothes; his appearance may have been modest; often he had a leaning toward alcoholism—trying to avoid through alcohol the tremendous tension inevitably suffered by a man constantly experiencing both poles of the archetype. But he had no delusions of grandeur; he is for us an image of the good wounded healer.

Those of conservative temperament may be inclined to believe that the modern physician is in particular danger of being unable to experience the whole archetype. At first glance he may seem like a specialized technician doing assembly line work in a hospital. It may seem that the old doctor was the wounded healer *par excellence,* but the modern, technically oriented specialist tends to fend off one pole of the archetype. However the archetype operates in the greatest variety of ways. It is inner reality as well as outer. The medicine man in the bush had his own methods, which were not comparable to those of the educated doctor in ancient Greece. The medieval physician, doling out Arab potions, in turn worked in a manner entirely different from that of the nineteenth century family doctor making his rounds in horse and buggy. The surgeon in the First and Second World Wars had his own way of living the archetype, and the highly trained specialist at the Mayo Clinic equally has his own particular way of operating. But all of these, regardless of how divergent their techniques and methods may be, can nevertheless either live the entire archetype or repress one of its poles. They can all be wounded healers or petty tyrants. Which one comes to the fore depends not on whether they are a nineteenth century family doctor or a narrowly specialized staff member in a modern hospital. The splitting of the archetype is an inner event, depending less on the external situation than on the doctor's own psychological development and capacities.

To further clarify what I am trying to say I should like to refer to one last image, though fully aware that it may be impertinent: that of Christ. Jesus Christ is an historical and religious reality, and therefore only with the greatest reservations is he to be understood as a psychological symbol. But where better than in him can we see the wounded healer? He was not only a healer of sickness on the physical level but a healer of man's existential sickness in sin and death.

Jesus Christ was wounded and bore the sins of humanity. He came to heal the world of sin and death, yet he bore all sins and had to die. He refused ever to make use of power, acknowledging only God his father as powerful. Thus he is the wounded healer in the highest sense. By comparison the physician is a mere dwarf who throws himself into the struggle between life and death, sickness and health. But the doctor can only work creatively if he bears in mind that despite all his knowledge and technique, in the final analysis, he must always strive to constellate the healing factor in the patient. Without this he can accomplish nothing. And he can only activate this healing factor if he bears sickness as an existential possibility within himself. He is less effective when he tries to unite the two poles of the archetype through petty power. But even then he will be more effective than if he completely ignores or cannot grasp the significance of this split in the archetype.

CHAPTER FOURTEEN
Physician, Psychotherapist,
Social Worker, and Teacher

In the last chapter I tried to deal with the archetypal problems of the medical profession. Its basic model is also of importance for certain non-medical ministering professions. Some of these have departed from medicine without completely losing their doctor-like character, while others have turned increasingly toward the medical model often having had too little contact with it in the past. The fundamental healing character of psychotherapeutic and analytical work has led to certain misunderstandings in recent times. Some in the field have advanced the view that only trained physicians should be permitted to function as psychotherapists. This view might better be expressed as only those who have been gripped by the archetype of the "wounded healer" should be psychotherapists. When medical doctors had difficulty accepting that the basic physician's attitude may also be found in people with no medical training, non-medical psychotherapists and analysts began to defend themselves. One view advanced was that the non-medical psychotherapists should adhere to a different model than the doctor. Their chief concern, it was said, was not sickness and health but the soul. The non-medical psychotherapist and analyst should not primarily aim at bringing the patient to health; their responsibility was for the "salvation" of the psyche. Just as the ego and the self are sometimes opposed and do not always pursue the same goals—so goes the argument—

general health and "salvation of the soul" are not always identical. The medically oriented therapist merely tries to help the patient to a state of health, while the psychologically oriented therapist has the task of helping the psyche move toward the self, toward meaning.

This view seems questionable to me. Every person must search for the so-called meaning of life, for his life plan, and can be helped by anyone else. This is not a closed field staked out for particular specialists. The wounded, the ill suffering from emotional difficulties, call for help; they wish to be healed to the point where they can continue to develop in keeping with their own potential. There are some individuals who are so fascinated by the eternal struggle between sickness and health that they feel called upon to take part in that battle. They do not wish to avoid it or merely suffer it passively.

Like the doctor, the psychotherapist, and the analyst, the modern social worker also has a healing aim. He feels obliged to improve and to heal "sick" social conditions. Thus, although he holds no medical diploma and his training has nothing whatever to do with medicine, the social worker's profession to a certain extent shares a common fate with that of the physician.

In these professions the problem of the split archetype appears—whether the polarity be healthy-sick, conscious-unconscious, socially sick-socially healthy. The power hungry doctor, the psychotherapist acting as a false prophet and quack, the social worker as an inquisitor, are all related in their archetypal problem-complex. All are fascinated by the "healer-patient" archetype, suffer from the two poles of this archetype, can function as the wounded healer, and may repress one pole of the archetype, project it, and thus fall into certain forms of the power drive.

ADOLF GUGGENBÜHL-CRAIG

The problem of the split archetype is also found in another field of activity which we must count among the ministering professions. I refer to that of teacher. The teacher-student encounter runs parallel to an inner tension between the states of being a knowledgeable adult and an unknowing child. In every adult there is a child who constantly leads us to new things. The adult's knowledge makes him rigid and inaccessible to innovation. The unknowing child's irrational experimentation, his naive openness, must be retained as a potential in every adult if he is to remain emotionally alive. Thus the adult is never completely grown up. If he is to be somewhat healthy psychically, he must always keep a certain childlike unknowingness.

Among the general public, school teachers are often accused of being infantile and unrealistic. This is not completely untrue. If one has many dealings with teachers, one is soon reluctantly forced to admit a certain childishness and infantilism in their behavior. There must, after all, be something in the state of childishness which fascinates the teacher or else how could he bear to spend his entire working time among children? A dynamic teacher must have a certain dynamic childishness in himself, just as a doctor must have a vital relationship to the pole of illness.

One often meets teachers who seem to have lost every trace of childishness, who have even fewer childish traits than the average healthy adult. Such teachers have become "only teachers," who confront unknowing children almost as their enemy. They complain that children know nothing and do not wish to learn; their nerves are torn by their students' childishness and lack of self-control. For this kind of teacher, children are the other, that which he himself wishes never to be. Such teachers derive a certain pleasure from demonstrating their power over children, tormenting them, and keeping them in line with carefully calculated mathematical "averages."

The archetype by which the good teacher is fascinated is that of the knowing adult-unknowing child. A good teacher must stimulate the knowing adult in each child, so to speak, just as the doctor must arouse the patient's inner healing factor. But this can only happen if the teacher does not lose touch with his own childishness. In practical terms this means, for example, that he must not lose spontaneity in his teaching and must let himself be guided somewhat by his own interests. He must not only transmit knowledge but also awaken a thirst for knowledge in the children. Yet this he can only do if the knowledge-hungry, spontaneous child is still alive within him. Unfortunately, modern school regimens and teaching plans use every possible means to destroy these spontaneous, childlike qualities, so the teaching archetype is split. The teacher's childishness is repressed and then projected onto the pupils. When this happens, learning progress is blocked. The children remain children, and the knowing adult is no longer constellated in them. The teacher becomes smarter and the pupils more stupid. Such a teacher, who has split off the childish pole of the archetype, then complains that his pupils used to be much more eager to learn. His contact with children is made only through power and discipline. At the same time he becomes bitter and saddened. The new, the fresh, the childishly enthusiastic in him has died. Children are his enemies, representing the internally split pole of the archetype whose reunification is attempted through power.

But in this book we are interested primarily in the therapist of the psyche. We have tried to illuminate the basic model behind his behavior. Many fundamental problems of his vocation apply to all the ministering professions, while others affect him alone. In order to understand his problems, now we must examine new psychological questions. As with the split archetype, we will approach our goal in a roundabout way. To come to grips with my chief concern, I must first deal with something completely different.

CHAPTER FIFTEEN
Shadow, Destructiveness, and Evil

Homo homini lupus

The destructive urge appears with notable openness during youth. In this phase of life, we can see it in its direct and undisguised form. Young people tend toward outbreaks of destructiveness and vandalism. They enjoy destroying property and endangering lives. We hear complaints of such youthful behavior from Capetown to Stockholm and from Moscow to Edinburgh. Nations in every stage of cultural and political development suffer from the destructive behavior of youth, which is often somewhat rationalized by political or social motives. The psychology of youth is therefore an appropriate field for examining the psychological background of the destructive urge in general.

The first thing evident about the destructive behavior of young people is that they wantonly destroy not only the lives and property of others but their own as well. The way youngsters drive their cars, for example, is often as suicidal as it is murderous. In other ways too, they repeatedly place themselves in situations and undertake acts of bravado which are in fact dangerous only to themselves. Young people are attracted by danger. There is no point in going into details here; reading the daily papers is enough.

Youth's destructive acts are often pigeonholed under the label, "Signs of our times." The blame is put on the breakdown of our values, sociological developments, and restructuring, the insecurity of modern humanity, etc. But we are unquestionably not dealing here with a "sign of the times." Destructiveness toward themselves and others has always been characteristic of youth. To phrase it rather extremely: throughout history young people have always been ready to kill and to die, for little or for nothing at all. Humanity's destructive wars have always found enthusiastic participants among the young. What is behind this destructiveness? How can it be explained psychologically?

It is an unpleasant task to deal with humanity's destructive urge. Hardly anyone will deny that people are destructive toward themselves and others. But there are a variety of explanations for this phenomenon.

Marxists, for example, regard humanity's (and youth's) destructive behavior as a result of class struggle, of suppression, and exploitation. This class struggle creates an atmosphere of hatred which inevitably leads to destructive behavior. But the Marxists believe that when the class struggle is finally over, and we have a classless society, people will no longer act destructively. Of course many destructive acts will be necessary to reach that point. But once reached, no more studies of destructiveness will be necessary, since the phenomenon itself will have disappeared.

The Marxist view is expressed, in milder form and in assorted variations, in many discussions about human destructiveness. The opinion is repeatedly put forward that this phenomenon is simply a consequence of false social organization, that humanity's destructive urge is the result of distorted sociological, political, and economic structures and can be eradicated through their elimination. So-called authoritarian upbringing is also blamed for human destructiveness and antiauthoritarian education is praised as the road to salvation.

Such attempted explanations might be termed "futurism," as British historian Arnold Toynbee used the word. The futurists believe that changes in society are possible which will do away with destructiveness. They are able to see a golden age of humanity beckoning in the future. The hard facts of reality today are recognized but denigrated as errors which can be avoided in times to come.

Herbert Marcuse also tries to deal with destructiveness on a sociological-futuristic basis. In his view, modern humanity is suppressed, exploited, manipulated, etc., by dark powers. Western humanity today believes he is free, but according to Marcuse, in reality he is a helpless slave whose material comfort gives him the illusion that he has a voice in events. Basically, however, modern humanity has been alienated from himself by the manipulation of society and lives in constant frustration, which explains his destructiveness. The way out of the present situation lies in the total destruction of the existing social structure. When it has been destroyed, a new, nondestructive, non-frustrated, happy humanity will be possible. Marcuse bases some of his views on Freud and accepts the latter's opinion that the more civilized we become, the less gratification is given to our instincts. Man's social and cultural development demands a sacrifice of instinct. Frustration is the result.

In his book, *On Aggression*, Konrad Lorenz, using zoological concepts as his tools, had also dealt with humanity's destructiveness. According to Lorenz, aggression is one of the fundamental instincts necessary for the survival of the individual and the species. Among predatory animals, aggression against members of the same species is coupled with inhibition. A wolf, who is defeated in battle, exposes his throat to his victorious fellow-wolf and is not killed by his conqueror.

The human creature was a harmless animal as long as he had no tools. No such built-in inhibition was needed. With the development of tools, however, humans gained the ability to kill one another. Their harmlessness disappeared; aggression was still there but no inhibition. Thus, according to Lorenz, destructiveness is basically an instinct which became dangerous to the human species due to altered conditions in the course of its development.

C. and W. M. S. Russel of England have another zoological explanation for the destructive aspect of human behavior. These authors maintain that destructiveness is a result of overpopulation. Certain apes, peaceable in their natural habitat, become aggressive and destructive when penned closely together in a zoo, even attacking their own young. An excessively constricted territory confuses the instincts, resulting in a constant stimulation of aggression.

There are limits to the validity of zoological attempts to explain human behavior. We can understand animals only from the outside, but humans, since we are such ourselves, can be understood, somewhat, from within. There are inherent limits to our understanding of animal behavior, and therefore it is questionable to what extent we may draw from this limited understanding valid conclusions about the human condition.

Moreover, all zoological explanations ignore the fact that human aggression, such as the classic example of youthful behavior, is generally coupled with self-destructive acts. This fact has also been ignored by most psychologists— although not by all, as we will see later. Yet what can Jungian psychology offer by way of explaining humanity's destructive behavior?

Jung made an interesting attempt at explaining this with the concept of the "shadow," which we mentioned earlier.

He did not always describe his insights systematically. He was not concerned with building a dogmatic, carefully constructed psychological system. I will try, in the following paragraphs, to present the concept of the shadow in a somewhat systematized form.

The so-called shadow consists of three diverse psychological structures which are closely interrelated. The first is the *personal shadow*. To a certain extent this is congruent with Freud's concept of the unconscious. It embraces images, fantasies, drives, experiences which have had to be repressed for personal reasons in the course of an individual's history. The taboos imposed by parents, for example, often force children to repress certain things. The contents of the personal shadow are frequently harmless in themselves; they are often certain aspects of sexuality which are regarded by the parents or the environment as negative and not permissible. The personal shadow also contains many unpleasant personal experiences which the ego or the superego prefers to forget. The modern Western European's personal shadow often includes certain sexual perversions and a great deal of repressed aggression.

The personal shadow is closely linked to the so-called *collective shadow*. Within a given collectivity, the collective shadow is the same. That is, in each individual, it contains all that is not acceptable in the cultural milieu to which that individual belongs. The collective shadow is the dark other side of the collective ideal. The general European ideal of the nineteenth century, for example, was a mixture of Christianity and liberalism; love, progress, purity, friendliness, sobriety, chastity, etc., were the collective values. The collective shadow of that epoch therefore contained hatred, Dionysian ecstasy, orgiastic tendencies, sexuality as an end in itself, lust, etc. During the antisexual era of Queen Victoria, the collective shadow showed itself in the blossoming of prostitution and pornography.

A good way to become familiar with the collective shadow of the Christian Church from the Middle Ages to the modern era is by studying the history of the Jews or the phenomenon of the witch hunts. If we are interested in the collective shadow of nineteenth century England, it is worthwhile studying the history of famine in Ireland or the expulsion of the Scottish Highlanders. In this way we can learn about the dark side of the official ideals of the British ruling class—brutality, power, and greed.

The personal shadow works destructively against ego-ideals; the collective shadow tries to demolish collective ideals. Both these shadows also have a valuable function. Both ego and collective ideals must be repeatedly subjected to attack, since they are false and one-sided. Were they not continually being eaten into from the depths of the human soul, there would be neither individual nor collective development.

Linked with these two kinds of shadow and providing them with energy, yet fundamentally different, is the so-called *archetypal shadow*. Here the word shadow is actually misplaced. Graphically speaking, shadow is something secondary, since it is light which creates shadow. Conscious personal and collective ideals have their shadows, their dark other sides. In this sense the individual and collective shadows are not really independent. But the case of the archetypal shadow is different. A better word for it might be simply "evil," although this word conjures up too many collective moral associations.

Jung conceived of evil as something independent and not, for example, as a *privatio bond,* merely the absence of good. In his terms it may be understood as "the murderer and suicide within us." This archetypal shadow is an inherent mode of human behavior—an archetype. In the course of history it has been represented by such symbols as the Devil or the alchemists' *sol niger* (black sun). Many of the more frightful gods and goddesses in religious history are symbols of this archetypal shadow: Shiva, Loki, Beelzebub.

In his book, *Beyond the Pleasure Principle*, Freud describes something similar. On the basis of experiences during World War I, Freud came to the conclusion that humanity is fundamentally guided by two instincts or drives: Thanatos, the death instinct, and Eros, the life instinct. Freud recognized the connection between aggression directed at others and that directed against oneself. The death instinct is the "longing" and drive toward death, toward the destruction of ourselves and others. Freud was not able to reduce this primary destructive urge to anything else. Both Freud and Jung recognized this "murderer and suicide in us" as something which is simply there and cannot be conjured away by any sort of theorizing.

As I mentioned recently, the figure of the Devil is partly a symbol of the archetypal shadow. So it is worth taking a look at fairy tales or myths in which both the Devil and a youth appear. One such case is the Grimm fairy tale "The Devil With the Golden Hair." The hero of this story, in order to marry the princess, must tear three golden hairs from the Devil's head and bring them back.

Marriage with the princess symbolizes the young man's development toward wholeness, toward an inner and outer unification with the feminine. But in order to reach this stage, he must make intimate contact with the Devil. The Devil has golden hair, and since gold is a symbol of light, of consciousness, the golden-haired Devil has an affinity with the Sun god; or he may also be characterized as

Lucifer, "bearer of light." Before his fall, Lucifer was one of the most luminous angels in the heavenly hosts. Our fairy tale seems to be trying to say that psychological development toward wholeness is only possible through increased consciousness by direct contact with evil. In other words a young person cannot continue to develop if he fails to come into contact with the archetypal shadow.

It is worth noting that the Devil, although he stands for evil symbolically, is frequently also understood as a servant of God. In the *Book of Job*, Satan is still one of God's sons. And in *Isaiah* 45:7 we read: "I form the light, and create darkness: I make peace, and create evil: I the Lord do all these things."

Mythology tries to provide answers to psychological, philosophical, and religious questions for which we cannot find rational solutions. The inexplicable, the mysterious, is expressed in mythological symbols. It is indeed difficult, if not impossible, to explain by rational psychological means why a youngster must enter into a relationship with the archetypal shadow in order to further his own development. In trying to deal with this question, despite its difficulty, we must remain aware of our own limitations.

Our human attitude toward ourselves, our world, toward all of Creation and to God, has a rather strange aspect. We want to have a certain degree of freedom, we wish to judge, to evaluate, to take a stand, to view things from all sides, and make our decisions freely. We not only want to know what is right and wrong, like Adam and Eve who ate the fruit of the Tree of Knowledge; we also want freely to decide what it is we wish to do. We strive to find our own standpoint from which to judge the world, God, and our fellow humans. If we cast our lot for life, we want to do so more or less voluntarily.

SHADOW, DESTRUCTIVENESS, AND EVIL

But only he who is capable of saying "No" to the world is also capable of affirming it. Only he who has the freedom to destroy can freely turn to the world with love. Without the possibility of the sinful, destructive "No," we would be as we imagine the animals to be: we would simply exist, driven by our survival instinct, without any possibility of decision, without any sense of freedom. We would have no opportunity to evaluate, to become conscious, and to choose. The existence of the archetypal shadow may be a specific human attribute.

A young person is in a transitional state between childhood and adulthood. Of course the child has ample destructiveness in him; many children act like devils incarnate. But a child's overall situation is largely determined by his parents. In wrestling with his problems, he uses tools, images, and attitudes given to him by his parents. Thus, in many respects, the child is not free. An adult is naturally also formed by his parents; most of his attitudes have simply been taken over from them. But, in order to develop psychologically, the adult must pass through a phase of denial and destruction so that he can then, voluntarily, so to speak, further cultivate his parents' values or find new ones for himself. A youth making the transition from childhood to adulthood must make contact with the Devil, with destructiveness. He must also experience the possibility of destroying to fight his way through to freedom.

In a certain respect I am now trying to make the existence of the archetypal shadow understandable, and in the process I am diluting it somewhat. My conceptualizing and explanations are only of limited worth. We can to a certain extent try to understand the meaning of this murderer and self-murderer within us, as I have attempted to do, but at the same time, we have no alternative but to regard this dark side of ourselves as something inexplicable, to recognize it as such, and to guard ourselves against it. We cannot really say whether the purpose of this "No" to creation is really only to give us freedom.

Perhaps it is no mere accident that in many primitive initiation rituals, a youngster is required to engage in something destructive, whether by exposing himself to severe danger or by killing and cutting off the head of an enemy.

Young people must have contact with the Devil, but they must on no account identify with him. A youth's ego must remain somewhat removed and aware of what it is doing. In most cases, when healthy youngsters destroy property, steal, or let themselves in for other destructive activities, they know that they are involved in an experiment. They are aware that their actions, though interesting, are really "bad."

A certain qualification is needed at this point. Not all youngsters engage in openly destructive behavior; not all drive their cars suicidally or become involved in riots. A direct living out of evil is just one way of contacting evil. Another is by fantasying, or by identifying with the fantasies of another. Schiller was a youngster when he wrote *The Robbers*. Goethe vented his own suicidal impulses by writing *Sorrows of Young Werther.* Literature is full of dark figures with whom a reader can identify and who can help contact one's dark side. Motion pictures, television, and theater give countless opportunities to steal some of the Devil's golden hairs through identification with manifestations of destructiveness. Destructive fantasies are important in young people, whose daydreams are often filled with ideas of suicide, murderous impulses, and the most grizzly, destructive acts.

SHADOW, DESTRUCTIVENESS, AND EVIL

Some young people are able to contact destructiveness through philosophizing or to touch the Devil through religious art. But far too many youngsters fail tragically in their bold endeavors to tear a few golden hairs from the Devil's head. Destructiveness—evil per se—is exceedingly uncanny and unbearable to everyone. The natural thing is to push it away, and get rid of it somehow. For this reason many young people, when they are in the stage of their *Auseinandersetzung* with evil, show a tendency to project the archetypal shadow. When this happens they experience adults, parents, the "older generation," as evil and destructiveness incarnate. After a time a healthy youth withdraws these projections. But there are those who grow up in an environment which seems highly destructive and filled with hate. Perhaps the mother has rejected the child, or even given it away; there may be a lack of a proper family life; the parents may remain strange, remote, alien to the child. Coming from a disadvantaged background, such a child may have had difficulties in school, may have been rejected by teachers and classmates. But whatever the specifics, there are cases in which a young person has in fact experienced a great deal of destructiveness from his environment. Growing into adolescence, into the stage where contact must be made with evil, it is naturally quite easy to try to simplify the conflict by projecting destructiveness on the environment or at least on a part of it. To such a young person, evil is now not an integral part of human psychology but only a characteristic of the environment, of certain people, and social structures. Such projections block all further personal psychic development and make social integration exceedingly difficult. Everything negative that happens is understood as being caused by the wicked outside world, which must bear the blame for the youngster's own destructive and self-destructive behavior. The youth rationalizes his self-destructiveness by saying something like: "This is what the world wants, and this is what it'll get—with a vengeance!"

Such attitudes are especially familiar to social workers. Faced with a youngster caught in this sort of pattern, the social worker can do anything, try anything, and it is all interpreted as malevolent. If he tries to find a job for the youth, he is accused of maliciously trying to rob him of his freedom and control his life. If the social worker deliberately refrains from trying to find him a position and insists that the youngster try to help himself, this is of course construed as an indication that the case worker does not want to help his charge and secretly hopes that he will never find work at all.

If such youngsters are rather introverted and able to experience some of their conflicts on the inner level, in fantasy, they may have a chance of just getting by, socially speaking, although perhaps with difficulty and bitterness. However in most instances these young people are not fortunate enough to grow up in an environment which stimulates the inner life and might provide them with the tools necessary to confront their problems on the level of fantasy and symbol. Therefore they are often prone to live out whatever is going on inside them.

And then we are faced with the classic case of the neglected, antisocial, perhaps even criminal "juvenile." On the surface his destructive acts are similar to those of the youngster who is experiencing only momentary contact with the destructive, but on the inner level the situation is different. For this person the contact with the Devil, with the destructive, becomes a tragedy, a quixotic battle with an environment which is seen as a personification of evil.

Both as juveniles and in later life, antisocial types of this kind are often mistakenly classified as psychopaths, as individuals with inborn character defects. If, as adults, they succeed in starting a family, they often instill a genuinely antisocial attitude in their children, which encourages them to project and thus makes it more difficult for them to work through their own problems. The situation can become particularly grave when these individuals also happen to be members of unpopular racial or ethnic minorities.

This kind of chronic decay is extremely tragic—because only people who have a certain psychological differentiation can fall victim to it. The indifferent and dull witted do not react that way even to rejecting and destructive environments. The phenomenon of evil and the destructive does not present them with any great problems. They merely come into superficial contact with it in youth and then go on to lead their dull lives. Precisely those who, even as children, were deeply impressed by evil fall into this deadly trap as they grow up. They never give up the battle against evil—but theirs is a senseless struggle because they fail to see that, in the final analysis, the destructive is an inner problem, and the projection of this problem onto the outer world always creates new misery and suffering.

CHAPTER SIXTEEN
Is Analysis Condemned to Failure?

In the previous chapter I tried to illustrate the phenomenon of the shadow, particularly the archetypal shadow, in terms of youthful development. This archetypal shadow naturally continues to be a factor in all people, even after they have reached adulthood. The average healthy individual repeatedly falls victim to his own self-destructive and aggressive tendencies, destroying what he has built, sabotaging relationships which are important to him, tormenting his own family and friends—or shifting his destructiveness to his environment. But the psychotherapist is in a particularly unfortunate situation vis-a-vis this archetypal shadow. Earlier I mentioned the psychological "law" which states that the more we strive for something bright, the more its dark counterpart is constellated. I indicated that as a psychotherapist tries to become more conscious and to help his patients do the same, his unconscious side is constellated more powerfully than that of the average person's. This might be expressed in paradoxical terms as follows: the more conscious a psychotherapist becomes, the more unconscious he becomes; the more light is cast upon a dark corner of a room, the more the other corners appear to be in darkness.

However the most difficult thing for everyone is to become conscious of the workings of the archetypal shadow, of one's own destructive and self-destructive tendencies, and to experience them in oneself rather than only in projections. Thus the psychotherapist, who in a certain respect is a particularly unconscious individual, is subject even more than others to the archetypal shadow. The therapist's conscious efforts are directed at helping people by freeing them from their own destructiveness. For eight hours each day, he encounters people whom he wishes to lead away from destructiveness and back to health and joy in life. But this endeavor places excessive demands on him. So much conscious good will must constellate a roughly equal amount of unconscious evil intent and destructivity.

The dangers of the psychotherapeutic profession were recognized by its founders. This is why a thorough training analysis is required before a would-be therapist may begin his own analytical and therapeutic work. Extensive knowledge of psychology and psychopathology is also called for, so that the therapist can develop a delicate and differentiated feeling for that which is neurotic and "sick" in his patients and can unmask it. But it is precisely this knowledge which betrays the analyst into coolly and objectively tracking down the destructiveness in his patients, and with this same objectivity, cutting off access to his own dark aspects, seeing them only in others.

Every day the psychotherapist is confronted with uncommon behavior, outbreaks and expressions of the personal, collective and archetypal shadows. The patients who come to him are seeking help with their destructive behavior. It is these which comprise the psychotherapist's daily working environment. So it may happen that the therapist comes to see the functioning of the archetypal shadow, for example, only in his environment, like the chronically neglected juvenile we described earlier. He sees so much of these phenomena that he no longer has the strength to recognize and continue to study them in himself.

Another complicating factor is that many schools of psychotherapy have a severe inclination to avoid the confrontation with archetypal destructiveness. They try to make of psychology a "natural science," believing that the psychotherapeutic process can be mechanized and that the psychological processes in oneself and in others can be studied by objective observers, like a chemist objectively studies a chemical reaction. Even Freudians, for instance, have difficulty tracking down in themselves what Freud described as the death instinct (Thanatos), since it is a frightening phenomenon and may destroy their objective scientific attitude.

In Jungian psychotherapy emphasis is placed on the shadow problem. But only the personal and collective shadows are examined, which are the dark sides of collective and ego ideals. Yet the archetypal shadow is frequently ignored.

As I have already said, the psychotherapist is in a difficult and dangerous psychological situation, from whichever side we examine his problems. To the extent that his basic model is that of the physician, he is subjected to the temptation of repressing one pole of the healer-patient archetype and projecting it onto his patients. As is often the case with doctors, the exercise of power here represents an attempt to heal this split. The healer-patient polarity is further heightened by that of consciousness-unconsciousness. Unconsciousness is projected onto the patient, while the analyst, whose task it is to bring his patients to greater consciousness, unjustifiably seems to himself to be a particularly conscious individual. But even if he partly attains genuine consciousness, he cannot avoid a deepening of the shadows in his own unconscious. And within this darkness function the dark brothers of the priest and the doctor, to whom the therapist is related—that is the false prophet and charlatan. This psychological situation provides an ideal field of operation for the archetypal shadow. Destructiveness makes use of the split in the archetype and of the dark figures of charlatan and false prophet. Thus the analyst is threatened on every side.

By this time the reader may be wondering if the entire undertaking of psychotherapy is condemned to failure from the outset, or at best, only feasible for psychological geniuses. Many therapists who are aware of this complex problem form comfort from the naive belief that they can master the situation through a careful training analysis and subsequently a conscientious examination of their own unconscious. But I do not believe this view to be tenable. I sometimes hear colleagues express the opinion that these dangers can be avoided if the psychotherapist carefully records and studies his own dreams. The difficulty here is that, in such a case, the dreams must be interpreted by the dreamer himself. Yet there is no system, no objective technique, for understanding the messages of dreams. Dream interpretation is a creative, almost an artistic activity. In the final analysis the interpretation of a dream depends on the interpreter. In time, the experienced therapist develops great skill in interpreting his own dreams according to his own wishes. He recognizes shadow phenomena in himself only when it suits his ego to do so, and he may even misinterpret them as bright aspects.

My remarks seem to be growing pessimistic. Yet they would appear to be confirmed by the countless, bitter disputes among psychotherapists. There are few fields in which internal conflicts are fought in a more unfair, unconscious, and destructive manner than among "officially" analyzed and allegedly "conscious" psychotherapists.

IS ANALYSIS CONDEMNED TO FAILURE?

Is psychotherapy, and particularly the analysis of the deeper strata of the human soul, an impossible undertaking? Must this splendid experiment be regarded as a failure? Are analysts bound sooner or later to find themselves in a blind alley?

CHAPTER SEVENTEEN
Analysis Does Not Help

I am trying in this book to show the difficult, problematical aspects of the psychotherapeutic profession. As a result I have been more or less ignoring the special, positive potential inherent in it. It hardly needs saying, despite the threat from the pitfalls we have been discussing, that many psychotherapists do excellent work and help countless people to find release from severe suffering. There are, certainly, some therapists who are not up to dealing with these dangers and thus actually do damage. But this naturally does not cast any serious doubt on the value of the profession itself.

I do not wish to confine myself in this book to highlighting dangers. I should also like to indicate possible ways of meeting them. Earlier I described how, in patient and analyst alike, forces are constellated which are hostile to the progress of an analysis. I also stated that it is therefore essential for the analyst to be open and honest toward himself, and in a certain sense, toward the patient so that these negative phenomena may be dealt with jointly. This may provide a starting point from which destructiveness can be countered. But there is a limit to such possibilities.

The great curse of the psychotherapist is his isolation. Most psychotherapeutic schools are admittedly strict in insisting upon a training analysis. They also require that a student analyst have his work controlled by an experienced colleague. But ultimately, the analyst in his work is completely dependent upon himself. Only he and his patients know what takes place in each hour. Increasingly, the analyst lives alone in a kind of tower. Many therapists are even alone when with their patients; all attempts by the patient to penetrate beyond the therapist's mask to his personality, perhaps to attack him, are repelled and interpreted as the patient's own problems. The personal style and theoretical views of many analysts make it impossible for them to be fundamentally called into question even by their patients. With reference to this point, Jung always clearly emphasized that the analytical process must be a mutual one, with analyst and patient each having an effect upon the other. But, like his colleagues of other schools, the Jungian analyst cannot escape the fact that analysis is an asymmetrical relationship. And it becomes progressively more asymmetrical as the analyst gains in age and experience, so that the patient's challenge to the psychic processes in the analyst becomes smaller. The split in the archetype—on the one hand the healthy doctor and on the other the sick patient—makes the dialogue between them increasingly more difficult. What the patient gives of himself becomes the other, something which ultimately no longer touches the analyst.

However there are genuine "wounded healers" among analysts; they are therapists in whom the archetype is not split. They are, so to speak, constantly analyzed and enlightened by their patients. Such an analyst recognizes how the patient's difficulties constellate his own problems, and vice versa, and he therefore works openly not only on the patient but on himself. He remains forever a patient as well as a healer. Unfortunately, this is all too often not the case; instead the analyst falls more and more into the role of only the healer, and hence the false prophet and charlatan.

ANALYSIS DOES NOT HELP

At this point one might voice the demand that an analyst should have his work controlled by a colleague throughout his career. But the word "control" is unfortunate. The so-called control analyses which are a standard part of the analyst's training are themselves full of questionable elements. Even the most honest young analyst cannot report during a "control session" every word, every gesture, and mood which occurred during his work with any given patient. He selects—and his selection is determined by the impression he wishes to make on his controlling analyst. Moreover, there are some dreams which cannot even be grasped by the controlling analyst since they may contain a message intended for the patient and his therapist but not for the controlling analyst. Analysis is such an intensely personal affair that it is easy for an outsider, using his own personal equation, to misunderstand what is going on. Suggestions made by controlling analysts are often blatantly wrong. All the dangers which I have previously described are related to therapy and can do damage, but they are always linked to the overall personal development of the analyst himself. Basically, then, a prime concern must be to find ways and means for repeatedly rousing and penetrating the analyst.

It has sometimes been suggested that analysts should undergo "training analysis" during their professional careers. But many objections can be raised to this idea. Only in a large city is it possible for one analyst to find another of the same school with whom he is not somehow involved politically, whether in a professional organization or in the academic realm. And a man with an official position can hardly express himself freely and openly to a colleague in a similar or equal position. There is too much potential rivalry standing in the way of a genuine contact.

At the same time, an older man would find it difficult to go for such a "training analysis" to a much younger colleague who is just beginning his professional career. It would be inadvisable for a young therapist, who is just beginning to develop his own practice, ᵗo continue being analyzed by an older colleague. This would raise the danger of his becoming fixed in the role of student or disciple.

Basically, all these attempts at finding a way to counter the dangers of the analytical profession through further analysis seem to me dubious, like Baron Munchhausen's effort to save himself and his horse from drowning in a swamp by pulling himself up by his own pigtail. All the dark phenomena of which I have spoken would again be constellated in such a new analysis and lead to further complications. Many analysts are capable of repeatedly working through and out of the shadow problems which arise in their analytical work. All analysts fall victim to these problems from time to time. But a good number become increasingly tangled in their own shadows in the course of the years. The more such problems are analyzed and reanalyzed, the stronger become the forces operating out of the shadows.

Joint discussion of cases with a group of colleagues is likewise of limited worth. Anyone who has taken part in such group discussions knows how little the heart of the analytical work is touched. Each participant in such a colloquium tries somehow to show up well in front of his colleagues, so that the collective situation always constellates intragroup rivalries. These can sometimes take strange forms. One therapist may wish to present himself as a particularly skillful analyst, and consciously or unconsciously, chooses the material which he brings to the discussion with this aim in mind. Another may try to appear as notably honest and self-critical, so that in presenting his cases, he may even paint himself as worse, more unconscious, and shadow ridden than he really is. Professional colloquiums of this kind are useful only for discussion of the general questions arising from the material presented.

Therapy groups consisting of professional analysts are also of limited value. The analytical shield of the participants is generally so dense that it cannot be penetrated.

Again we seem to be facing a stone wall. I want to emphasize once more that a many psychotherapists in their confrontation with their patients, and thus with themselves, are quite able to circumvent the professional pitfalls facing them. But many are simply unable to do so. And these latter cannot be helped by any of the countless possible (and impossible) varieties of reanalysis and case discussion. The patient comes as a suffering human being to the analyst. Often the patient can be helped, and after his therapy is ended, he can go on to healthy, independent development. Now and again there are therapeutic cases which require extremely long treatment. In such cases it is no longer a matter of leading the patient onward in his psychological development but rather of repeatedly saving him from breakdown. Here, too, the therapist can be helpful. But there would seem to be no help for the analyst himself in his professional shadow problems.

Perhaps the time has now come when analysts might in all humility look beyond their own profession for possible help in avoiding this tragic entanglement. A certain psychotherapeutic inflation may well be behind the effort to help the analyst by analytical means—as if analysis were the *non plus ultra* for the encouragement and stimulation of psychological development. And we are indeed talking here about psychological development, rather than the healing of neuroses. The therapist's entanglement in his own shadow is not an illness, and the therapist may not suffer directly from it. Doubtlessly he is less able to help his patients, and he may become less interesting as a person. But, to use the psychoanalytic terms coined by Freud, we might also say that this entrapment in the shadow represents an excellent ego defense and prevents a great deal of suffering and trouble. Because of the split archetype, destructiveness in the sense of the archetypal shadow, the unconscious, etc., is no longer primarily the therapist's problem. He has shaken it off and experiences it only in projections, so that by and large he enjoys something resembling inner peace. That something is not quite right in his own psyche may only be recognized from the fact that the family and close friends of such an "enlightened" therapist often find themselves in an odd state of confusion and chaos.

The solution to such difficulties cannot come from within. The more the analyst analyzes, examines, and follows the dictates of his unconscious, the more blind he becomes. He is merely confirmed in what he already knows. His blind spot prevents him from seeing the decisive dark areas of his own being, or if he grasps them intellectually, he is still not emotionally gripped by his self-knowledge.

CHAPTER EIGHTEEN
Eros

In order to break free of this vicious circle, the therapist must expose himself to something which touches
him deeply, something un-analytical (he is already too
much the master of analytical technique) which repeatedly
throws him off balance, stimulates him, shows him time
and again who he is, how weak and pompous, how vain
and narrow. It is surely not by chance that Socrates sang
the praises of friendship. In my opinion, and on the basis
of my experience, there is one thing which can ameliorate
or even dissolve the therapist's shadow-entanglement: friendship. At first glance this may seem rather banal. But it is
strange to see how this banality is over-looked by many
analysts. Friendship, loving but forceful encounters with
one's equals, to attack and be attacked, to insult and be
insulted—all of this strikes again and again at the psychic
center of those involved. What the analyst needs is sym-
metrical relationships; relationships with partners who are
up to his mark, friends who dare to attack him, to point out
not only his virtues but his ridiculous sides. This kind of
stimulation may be found with friends of the same sex. It
can also take place within a marriage—the depths of the
shadow must be plumbed in love. People not schooled
in analysis develop largely through intensive interpersonal
relations. The analyst has no choice but to do the same. It
is astounding to see how difficult many psychotherapists
find this. They may try to make so-called friends out of

their former patients, but the relationship to the patient naturally remains asymmetrical and one-sided even after the analysis is ended. Former patients, now "friends," cannot really get beyond the analyst's defense system. Many analysts maintain that they cultivate intensive friendships, when what they actually do is gather a circle of disciples around them and bask in the admiration. Many therapists even close themselves off from the psychological challenges presented by their own families. They begin to regard wife and children as analysands and to behave accordingly. Still other analysts destroy genuine friendships by transforming them into analytical relationships, avoiding the real problems of friendship through analytical and psychodynamic formulations. Friendship intensely lived—and intensely suffered—saves many a therapist from inextricable entanglement in his own dark and destructive side. Hatred and love flow back and forth between friends; love circles around the positive potential and hatred around the negative. An analyst without genuine friendships must have exceptionally great talent in order not to become rigid and alienated in his analytical work. But perhaps the word friendship is somewhat too limited. It might be better to say that the psychotherapist needs erotic confrontation outside the analytical framework.

Children, in their free and open development, can also penetrate to the analyst's shadow and drag it out into the light. The tragedy of childless therapists is not that their natural need for descendants remains unfulfilled, but that they miss the challenge which children offer.

We are dealing here with the fundamental problem of human development per se, with the difficulty of remaining open and vital throughout one's life. This is the theme elaborated repeatedly by Jung: individuation.

CHAPTER NINETEEN
Individuation

According to the writings of Jung, psychotherapeutic work has two main concerns. First to heal the analysand of neurotic or psychotic suffering, and second, to guide the process which Jung termed individuation. In his opinion most therapy at best ends with the healing, while individuation is a separate matter and does not automatically follow. It is difficult to define or describe individuation briefly. Pictures or images are needed to make it comprehensible. It is a matter of the fulfillment of human life, the flowering of the basic design of an individual human existence, the experience of individual meaningfulness. Individuation is not something which can be acquired and then securely owned. For the purposes of representation, it is symbolically described in such images as "the journey to the golden city." The efforts of the alchemists to transmute common substances into gold, their search for the Philosopher's Stone, are symbols of individuation projected onto matter. But the Philosopher's Stone can never be found any more than can the formula for turning base matter into gold. What is meant is the constant search for something, the intuiting of a goal without ever reaching it. Jung did not content himself with generalizations about this process but tried to come to grips with it more concretely. For instance he emphasized that in this respect it is important to experience human ambivalence, not to eliminate it but to "unite the opposites" on a higher plane. It is in this sense that he understood the alchemical symbols of the marriage of the King and Queen. He saw mandalas, the meditative images used by Tibetan monks which group the most varied opposites around a nuclear center, as symbolizing the goal of individuation. In religious terms, the process of individuation is often depicted by images of the "saving of the soul." The goal is to experience one's own soul as nearly as possible in its entirety, and in this sense to experience, most deeply, existential being as such, to accept and affirm it. Factors hostile to individuation are rigidity, closed-mindedness, a lack of openness to oneself and the world. The ways of individuation are strange and unique. They may lead through illness or health, through joy or misfortune. Individuation is the effort to contact the divine spark in humanity, to subject the ego to the Self.

Since individuation is not reconcilable with psychic narrowness, even the most unpleasant basic facts of existence must be taken into account. The shadow, fundamental destructiveness, must somehow be seen. A confrontation with death must occur. Jung's writings sometimes indicate that individuation takes place in the second half of life. Jung did not maintain this point dogmatically, but some of his followers have elevated it to a dogma.

In depth analysis, dreams and other expressions of the unconscious often point to an individuation process. They may show whether or not the person in question is seeking the Philosopher's Stone, or whether he is on a journey to the golden city. In my analytical experience, I have found that the individuation process may appear at any stage of life. I have often been able to observe it in young people, many of whom wrestle with the problems of God, death, and the Devil. Such young people are completely open to the overall polarity of human existence without being broken by it. They penetrate psychologically to the depths of the nature of humanity and Creation. I have recognized in the dreams of such adolescents the symbols of individuation and the finding of the Self, and I have seen how they confront and are influenced by these symbols.

On careful examination, the idea that only older people can penetrate to the heart of human existence is a rather strange one. Throughout most of human history, people have died relatively young. Even today in underdeveloped countries, most people do not live beyond the age of forty. How could it be that only those who, by good fortune, have been permitted to live more than thirty or forty years can have a chance of fulfilling their human destiny? Also, it should be noted that a large part of humanity's creative work has been done by men and women under forty.

The individuation process is related in a way to religious development. But to maintain that only people over forty are open to religious insights and experience is obviously false. At first glance there may be something attractive in the idea that it is the task of the young person to master the outside world, to establish himself professionally, found a family, etc., while that of the older is to turn his attention to the question of meaning. This view imposes a certain order and programmatic sequence on life, more or less approximating the model of a course of study. But perhaps in this case our thinking is excessively influenced by the image of school years and student life. An approach to the Self can take place at any age: a sixteen year old may be quite far along the path of individuation, while a sixty year old may have completely abandoned the search. Throughout our lives we draw nearer to the center of our being only to fall back from it again. This is a constant process; a cyclical approach and withdrawal. No person—and thus no analyst—can ever say of himself that he is now individuated and therefore, so to speak, "saved."

To prevent misunderstandings, I wish to emphasize again that the individuation process is not a phenomenon which runs parallel to mental and spiritual health. A person may be remarkably free of neurotic and psychotic symptoms and yet hardly touched at all by the individuation process. An ego may be strong enough to build effective defense mechanisms against humanity's greatest questions and deepest fears. Death may be set aside as something that happens to others but for the time being need not be considered by oneself. A strong ego can hide behind a practical view of life which is not willing to concern itself with anything ominous that cannot be changed, such as death. Shadow problems can be repressed or projected onto others. All our deeper fears can be shoved aside through apparently meaningful industriousness. One can set oneself partial goals, and in the striving for these side-step the question of general or overriding meaning. There are ample goals to be pursued: earning money, fulfilling family obligations, achieving a certain social status, smooth adjustment to one's social system, the diligent practice of a profession, the maintenance of physical health, etc.

There are of course many and varied ways of stimulating individuation in oneself and in others. In the writings of Jung, and even more in those of his followers, we learn that analysis is the modern way *par excellence* to promote individuation. The detailed dealing with the expressions of one's own unconscious within the framework of an intimate relationship, the striving for a positive attitude toward these expressions of the unconscious, the comprehending of one's own psychic life in terms of analytical psychology—all of these are of decisive importance. Thus it is understandable that an older analyst, a person in the second half of life who is constantly concerned with analysis and also tries to understand himself in terms of the categories of analytical psychology, should begin to think that he is, so to speak, a specialist in individuation and certainly well on the way to achieving it himself. He is reinforced in this inflated attitude by his patients who, for various reasons, wish to see in him someone who is not only psychically healthy but is far along on the path to individuation. In other words, they want their therapist to be an omniscient magician.

It might appear as if Jungian analysts are especially prone to a certain blind hybris. It is, after all, primarily in Jungian psychology that the terms "individuation" and "the second half of life" are given such importance and are liable to become dangerous in the ways I have described. But analysts of other schools as well, to whom the concept of individuation means nothing, for whom analysis is purely a way to mental health, and who reject everything else as metaphysical speculation—even these other analysts are liable to see analysis, in their own way, as the sole path to salvation. They, too, believe that their psychology and their therapeutic methods represent the means for humanity's redemption. An internationally prominent Freudian psychoanalyst once told me in all seriousness that World War II would not have happened if there had been more psychoanalysts in pre-war Germany, and if Freud's teachings had been more deeply lodged in the consciousness of the people. Analysts of every school are tempted to believe that they have found the key to humanity's deepest problems. This inflation even affects psychiatrists who do not use the methods of depth psychology. The attempt is often made to reduce the major phenomena of human history to the categories of psychopathology. Christ is pictured as a paranoid masochist, the saints become sexual neurotics. That many analytical schools do not recognize the difference between mental health and individuation may even heighten the danger of falling into a prophetic inflation. The analyst who has some successful "cures" behind him believes that he has helped people to find salvation—or at least that he knows how to do so. By not recognizing the difference between the concepts of mental health and individuation, he lacks the means of preventing an inner, psychological contamination of the two concepts and thus falls into a prophetic inflation.

CHAPTER TWENTY
The Helpless Psychotherapist

An image is slowly coming into focus of the experienced psychotherapist in the second half of life who has done excellent work and has mastered the theoretical and practical aspects of his field. Analysis, and the knowledge and techniques used in analysis, takes on increasingly wider significance for him. To the Jungian therapist this analysis is the great path not only to mental health but also to the soul's salvation. For the analysts of other schools all problems, if they are solvable at all, can be solved on the basis of analytical knowledge. All relationships, all friendships, and familial ties, art, social life, everything is narrowed down to the analytical and psychological. The analyst is no longer open to "being" in the existentialist sense but has withdrawn to an ivory tower and experiences the world only from that vantage point. And now there begins the tragic development which I have tried to depict in these pages; the serpent begins to consume itself by swallowing its own tail. The therapist increasingly falls victim to the shadow phenomenon. He becomes less effective as an analyst but believes that his effectiveness is growing. He deceives himself more and more, but he continues to be respected as a specialist, becomes neither unhappy nor neurotic nor psychotic. And ultimately he will die as a mentally sound, socially adjusted, and successful individual.

Earlier I indicated that friendship (erotic encounter), offers one way for the analyst to break out of this vicious circle. When I first mentioned this point, it was merely an unsupported premise. Before I return to it, I must digress a bit further.

Individuation is possible for any person at any age. It is a task for everyone. There is an Indian meditation scroll which shows Tsong Khapa, the founder of the Yellow Church of Tibet, surrounded by eighty-four Indian holy men (*mahasiddhas*) who have approached religious perfection. These *mahasiddhas*, whose lives are know to us from legends, attained their goal via all possible routes, as monk and as fool, as dancer and glutton, as crown prince or sluggard. What is expressed on this meditation scroll also applies to individuation in the Jungian sense. It would be grotesque to create such a scroll with a mere eighty-four analysts or analysands. Some disciples of Jung have certainly gone too far in asserting that the "true path" to individuation must somehow be via analysis. They have even gone too far in believing that, while an actual analysis may not be necessary, the tools and principles of analytical psychology are essential for a thorough grasp of ourselves. Individuation can take place in analysis, in the family, in our daily work, in artistic and technical endeavors—everywhere. One can use a thousand media to confront the fundamental problems of human existence. Or, to use religious terms, one may serve God in many ways. The juggler in the medieval legend who performed his art in the church before the Madonna was serving in his own way.

Of course most professional activities can be practiced effectively without the individuation process being activated. A mentally healthy insurance actuary who is rigid in his attitudes, no longer open to the world, no longer individuating, can certainly do his job well. But in all those occupations which have a decisive influence on other people, where our psyche is our principle working tool, the psychic attitude is naturally of paramount importance. The profession of psychotherapist is one such. The therapist not only uses certain technical methods, it is in the final analysis his own personality which has an effect on the patient. The analyst I described earlier who is constantly led by his shadow, without his knowing it and without suffering for it, is in no way neurotic or psychotic. In his own way he has found a *modus vivendi* with the demonic forces which permits him to lead a tension free, satisfied life. To a limited degree, he may even succeed in helping an occasional patient achieve a similar healthy stability. Many of his patients, after completing their analysis, are less plagued by neurotic symptoms, but they also tend to be somewhat less interesting as people and often even more egoistic and malicious. Something has been stopped: the process of individuation. The analyst who is no longer open, who has integrated his shadow so to speak, partly by living it out unconsciously and partly through projection, can no longer stimulate his patients to develop an understanding of individuation.

Jung points out again and again that an analyst can bring his patients no further than he himself has gone. This naturally does not apply to specific neurotic symptoms. A therapist may himself suffer from certain neurotic compulsions and yet succeed in freeing his patients from similar afflictions. But he can seldom stimulate an individuation process if he has closed himself off from it. And, as we have seen, part of the individuation process for the analyst is confrontation with the analytical shadow.

Only something non-analytical can occasionally break through this resistance. The psychotherapist must be challenged by something which cannot be either mastered or fended off by his analytical weapons and techniques. Works of art may shake one, the study of history may stimulate, an interest in natural science may lead to tortured questions. But the clever analyst finds it too easy to somehow press all such things into the analytical framework. An intelligent and differentiated analyst whom I know attended a very moving motion picture. But instead of yielding to the emotional experience, after the performance my colleague went into a long, ingenious, psychological analysis of the film. It is no rarity to see therapists who, when they might be deeply moved by a work of art, use psychological interpretation to fend off the experience of being moved. The Mona Lisa becomes just an "anima figure," modern paintings are seen as brimming with feminine and masculine sexual symbols.

Chapter Twenty - One
Eros Again

And so, as a last way out of the impasse, I come back to erotic relations with our fellow human beings. By erotic I do not mean sexual in particular but loving in the broadest sense. Friends both male and female, wives or husbands, brothers and sisters, children, relatives—all of these often have the power to challenge the analyst and the ability not to fall victim to his clever attempts at deterrence. And in such relationships shadow contents are constellated, since these people challenge the analyst from completely different sides and angles than do his patients. The therapist, however, can only fruitfully accept the challenge from love. Only then is he vulnerable. Professional colleagues can of course also have an effect on him to the extent that they are present not as analysts but as friends. But in these cases there must be awareness of the danger that therapist-friends often become therapist-accomplices, cleverly assisting in the battle against individuation, careful not to challenge the other in order not to be challenged themselves, and thus providing additional weapons against further psychological development.

A few examples would seem in order here to better illustrate what I have in mind. An analysts's wife complains to him one evening: "Lately you don't pay any attention when I talk. You seem to know it all already. And whenever we have guests, you act as if you know everything. I can never get a word in. If I start to tell a story you finish it for me or else you correct what I've said. And you're always interrupting the other women, too." These are not serious accusations, but they point to unpleasant traits of the husband. He can defend himself, of course, deny what his wife has said and try to insist that she is only projecting, etc. But his wife is, after all, not his patient; he cannot simply toss everything back into her lap. Finally all that is left for him is to confront his own dominating behavior and to feel regret at the pain he is causing. Such a confrontation can become complicated and difficult, but as he gradually begins to think more about himself, a small part of his shadow has been brought closer to home.

Another example is one day the friend of an analyst says to him, "I didn't much like the way you were behaving last night. You played up to Miss X like a peacock. You didn't even notice that she didn't give a damn about your ideas for reform at the university. She was just stringing you along." The analyst can try to defend himself against his friend's words, but he knows his friend is not just hostile and that there must be a kernel of truth in what he says.

These are quite harmless little conflicts, but they may suffice to show the direction in which things can go. An analyst may have the most serious confrontations with those close to him, and as long as he remains open within the love relationship, he must take these reactions seriously. This brings him into renewed contact with his own shadow. Contact with the shadow in private life also leads to contact with the professional shadow, and such confrontations can naturally also point to his positive sides.

This is all very well—but how does this activation and contact of the shadow stimulate the individuation process? It does so simply by bringing new movement to a psyche grown rigid. The soul opens up once again. This in itself does not necessarily trigger the individuation process, but it at least makes it possible once more.

New possibilities for movement in the analyst's psyche are naturally not only created by more or less harmless criticism from the people around him. The important thing is the involvement, the joy and sorrow, the disappointment and surprise, which flows back and forth between people who love one another. The experience of Eros between two people, and its fructifying effect on the psyche, cannot be described in dry psychological terms but only represented artistically. Once it has taken place, of course, it can again be put into analytical terms and grasped that way. But those psychological concepts must in turn be repeatedly relieved by the immediacy of erotic experience. And this can only be effective—fully and deeply effective—when it takes place between people who love each other, rather than between doctor and patient, analyst and analysand, or master and pupil.

But the psychotherapist is in a difficult position indeed; only to a slight degree can the study of the latest developments in psychotherapy help him to remain effective in his profession. He cannot prevent or ameliorate the splitting of the archetype by reading medical journals. His effectiveness depends to an overwhelming extent on the development of his own psyche. There may be other ways than friendship to safeguard him from the psychotherapist's shadow—but I have not found them yet. And even if they exist, they cannot be part of the analytical work. Certain forms of meditation might offer possible means. Unfortunately, however, most analysts, even if they try to deal with their inner lives contemplatively, are so caught in their analytical shadow that at best they find themselves on a treadmill. Perhaps there is a form of God oriented meditation which might free the analyst from the trap. But as a rule an intelligent and conscientious analyst has also included the religious sphere in the structure of his analytical world, or if he finds it somehow disturbing, can fend it off with analytical weapons.

The analyst's exposing himself to erotic relationships with the world around him does not mean simply that his emotional life must be somewhat stimulated. We are not dealing here with the contrast between intellectual understanding and emotional experience. Nor do we merely mean stimulating some feeling in the analyst in order to get his psychic development moving again. Our chief concern is overcoming the split in which he lives. The point is that he must actively, painfully, and joyfully come into direct contact in his dealings with humanity. He must somehow find a way to once more expose himself to the most difficult challenges. He must be shaken. The senile "I know, I know," must become the Socratic, "I don't know."

The profession of psychotherapist has many features in common with other occupations. What we have here termed the "helping professions" are all subject to a severe threat from the shadow. All people who believe they harbor a desire to help humanity must also be aware that the preoccupation with misfortune, social maladjustment, ignorance, illness, etc., constellates psychological problems in themselves. In the preparatory training for these professions, there is much talk of the difficulties created by "cases" and patients but hardly any mention of one's own dark sides. Part of the training of social workers, nurses, teachers, doctors, etc., should emphasize that the problems of the case or the patient are one's own as well. Like the English judge who, seeing a condemned murderer walking to the place of execution, spoke the immortal phrase: "There, but for the grace of God, go I." Students of the ministering professions should be informed in detail of the many ways in which the shadow sides of their chosen work can express themselves. There should no longer be well-educated social workers who believe in all seriousness that they can practice their profession like engineers, purely, technically, and objectively. There should be no teachers who think that only their pupils are childish, while they themselves have put all that behind them. As for doctors, it would be a great improvement to meet fewer of them who see illness only in their patients. These fundamental changes in attitudes pose tremendous challenges to educators in these fields.

But in the case of the psychotherapist, another particularly difficult factor complicates the picture. Depth psychology represents one of the modern ways to self-reflection and self-perception. Through the knowledge which it offers, and through analysis, the members of other ministering professions can receive help in their struggles with their own professional problems. A social worker, in order not to fall into his shadow, need not receive assistance from another social worker. He can turn to an analyst. A teacher need not look to another teacher in his school to help him in his own psychic development; a doctor need not necessarily become the patient of another doctor.

However the analyst becomes increasingly ossified and entangled in his own shadow by precisely that which can be of help to others—analysis and the knowledge of analytical psychology. The tools with which he can aid others may spell his own psychic doom. He can fend off all challenges. His patients are no match for him, and even the challenge of religion can be defeated by his mastery of analytical concepts. He has learned to encounter the unconscious, and he does so cleverly and prudently. Only through the emotional interchange with those to whom he stands in a relation of love can a new dimension be brought into his benumbed world. If he fails to achieve this, if he succeeds in using his psychology to drain and empty his interpersonal relations, he becomes a tragic figure.

But if he manages to open himself to this dimension of existence, then his development can proceed, and he becomes far more capable of helping his fellow men to free themselves from neurotic entanglement and to move along the path of individuation. He then becomes a true follower of the great founders of depth psychology. He is able to continue the confrontation with the deepest layers of the soul, begun in such a heroic fashion by Freud and Jung. He can live his own true destiny.

To be a psychotherapist is to exercise a specifically modern profession. It is an attempt to circumnavigate the world, to explore the psyche in its totality. Modern humanity's great adventure is not merely to explore the outer world; to an even greater extent it is to plumb the depths of the human soul. A psychotherapist who succeeds in avoiding the pitfall of the rigidifying split can perform an incalculable service for humanity and for himself. Analytical psychology has given him the knowledge with which he can, if he knows how to use it, open completely new dimensions for modern people. But he must wrestle with dark, uncanny forces in himself and in others. It is only through repeated confrontations with the shadow that he can fulfill his task. He cannot, like the biblical Isaac, spend just one night wrestling with the angel to win his blessing. His struggle for the blessing must last a lifetime.